moving TARGETS

CREATING ENGAGING BRANDS IN AN ON-DEMAND WORLD

GABRIEL ALUISY

shake press

Moving Targets
Creating Engaging Brands in an On-Demand World

© 2014, Gabriel Aluisy. All rights reserved.

Shake Creative
info@shaketampa.com

Although every precaution has been taken to verify the accuracy of the information contained herein, the author and publisher assume no responsibility for any errors or omissions. No liability is assumed for damages that may result from the use of information contained within.

Designations used by companies to distinguish their products are often claimed as trademarks. All brand names and product names used in this book are trade names, service marks, trademarks or registered trademarks of their respective owners. The publisher is not associated with any product or vendor mentioned in this book.

Edited by Stephen Hirst
Cover & interior design by Gabriel Aluisy

Library of Congress Control Number: 2014913182
ISBN: 978-0-9905832-0-2
10 9 8 7 6 5 4 3 2 1
1. Business & Economics 2. Advertising & Promotion
First Edition

Published by Shake Creative
shaketampa.com

Printed in the United States of America

CONTENTS

Introduction - Oops, Something Happened vii

Chapter 1 - On Demand, All the Time 1

Chapter 2 - Let's Get Personal 15

Chapter 3 - The Modern, Savvy Customer 19

Chapter 4 - Creating an Emotional Connection 25

Chapter 5 - Core Values, Creating the Seamless Experience 33

Chapter 6 - Competing on Value, Not Price 47

Chapter 7 - Defining Your Target Audience 57

Chapter 8 - Starting a Conversation 61

Chapter 9 - Speaking Your Customer's Language 67

Chapter 10 - Your Look Matters, Managing the Minutia 77

Chapter 11 - 7 Marketing Mistakes Brands Make 87

Chapter 12 - Branding a Lifestyle 91

Chapter 13 - Let's Play a Game 101

Chapter 14 - Stories Connect People 109

Chapter 15 - Building on a Strong Foundation 113

Chapter 16 - Zeroing In on Your Target 129

Chapter 17 - How to Devalue Your Brand 133

Chapter 18 - Reinvention the Right Way 137

Chapter 19 - The Brand Report Card 141

For Lucas

May you never cease to explore and create.

Acknowledgements

This book could not have been written without the support and guidance of family, friends and colleagues to whom I'm sincerely grateful. I would like to thank my wife, Ana, for her love, encouragement and incredible support while I wrote this. Stephen Hirst, for his editorial and narrative guidance. Chris Krimitsos and JP Grace for helping me secure valuable interviews for the book. Topher Morrison, Daniel Priestley, the team at Entrevo USA and KPI Tampa for inspiring me and holding me accountable. My father, Jonathan, for being an inspiration and teaching me to always finish what I start. My late mother, Roseann, for always encouraging my creativity as a child. Gary Teaney for his business guidance. Nick Friedman, Dave Hendricks, Joey Redner, and Ben Kosinski for letting me interview them and offering their expertise and advice. Belinda Vieira and Kelsey Farnell for their hard work at Shake while I finished this.

INTRODUCTION

OOPS, SOMETHING HAPPENED

Something remarkable happened in 2006 that ushered in an age of change. Like most revolutions or coups it started quietly and unassumingly. For some it was a simple phrase. For others it became a mantra. In the end—whether consciously or unconsciously—it would shape the way consumers interacted and endeared themselves to the products they used daily. Who would have guessed that a simple phrase could launch sweeping changes to the way corporations and small businesses alike built and maintained their brand identity?

I was sitting at my desk in Delray Beach, Florida when I noticed it for the first time. A few days prior, a co-worker had given me a gift. It was a virtual gift: one of his ten precious Gmail invites. At the time, Gmail was an invite-only service for techies and people in-the-know. I never would have guessed that invitation would launch my own passion for connecting brands to consumers.

I was pretty satisfied with my Hotmail account that I had used since 1999, as well as my company-provided Horde account. They were both a means to an end. Like most, I had never thought of email as anything more than a delivery system for electronic messages that had a finite limit to the information they could store.

Gmail was cool though. For one, it offered a limitless and constantly growing environment, where deleting emails was a thing of the past. I could save everything, until the end of time, on Google's dime! It also sported some great sorting options and had a built in chat system. I liked the way you could preview attachments without the need to download them and fish them out of a folder on your hard drive. Lastly, it was just an intuitive piece of software that worked nearly flawlessly.

It's that "nearly" bit that did it. Since it was so new, they were still working out some kinks. On that day I had just wanted to stop an outgoing email so I could edit a few lines of text. I hit the BACK button on my browser after I had hit SEND, but before I got the confirmation message that my email had gone through. That's when something came alive inside Gmail.

It felt like a scene out of *The Matrix* when I looked up to find that the system was speaking to me. Yes, the computer was talking back to me!

A little yellow box appeared on my screen telling me:

"Oops. Something went wrong."

Now, I wish I could tell you that at that moment I came to a great realization, trumpets sounded from heaven and my life was forever altered. The truth is, I muttered something under my breath like, "Damn it." I smirked at the quirkiness of that line, and went back to what I was doing. I re-wrote the email, more eloquently than the first draft (which is so often the case) and re-sent it.

I would see that message pop up from time to time in the next few days and weeks and slowly it began to take hold. I know I wasn't the only one that it affected. Since then, I have begun to see similar signs and messages from companies and brands that are on the cutting edge.

It seems ironic that a system flaw could signal such sweeping change to the thinking and philosophy of so many brands to come. But it did. This one little phrase would forever change "company speak".

CHAPTER 1

ON-DEMAND, ALL THE TIME

We live in an increasingly on-demand world where nearly everything is at our fingertips at the very instant we wish. We are consuming media at an exponentially faster clip, devouring music, books, DVDs, television, movies and more with ferocious hunger. As society's pace quickens, your brand must match it step-for-step.

Gone are the days of waiting for your favorite television show to air or re-run when you've missed it. Just use your DVR or a service like Hulu. Why bother calling into a radio request line when you can "YouTube it" and hear it right away? Better yet, services like Pandora or Spotify let you listen to it and then explore similar artists matched to your specific taste.

The album is officially dead and we've become a singles driven society where B-sides are replaced by the next big hit. There's never a need to wait for your local bookshop to open, because you can download a book straight to your Kindle or tablet in the time it would have taken you to brush your teeth and put your clothes on. Movies are just a few Netflix taps away—or if you're daring enough, you could download current releases over the internet. Just about every major network offers an app that lets you stream their content at your convenience.

This on-demand world is not limited to media outlets. Every business must learn to feed the ever-increasing need of instant gratification. Business-to-consumer brands feel the pressure of the pace most, but business-to-business companies are affected as well, because this is a worldwide psyche shift.

Since the gates of the information age opened, people have stampeded through like a herd of buffalo, squashing out brands that refuse to adapt—just ask Blockbuster or AltaVista. It's relentless too; they're not going to slow down. The pace only grows more furious.

The average consumer is developing a "give it to me now" mentality, and not just for their dry-cleaning. If you want your brand to succeed you had better be prepared to deliver instantly. People increasingly want an immediate solution to their problem. If your brand can solve that problem or answer a question quicker than the next, you've taken the first steps to success and will gain a valuable leg up on your competition.

It's not enough to be better than the next guy—your brand or product has to be better *and* faster. In 1993, the internet was running over telephone lines at 56k speed. Not even a decade passed before 50mb speeds and faster were available to households over fiber optic lines. That's about 200 times faster! Is your business 200 times faster than it was 10 years ago? Can you imagine a world where you're moving 200 times as fast as you are today? You had better, because in 5 years, you will probably need to be there. Businesses, therefore, need to make decisions, provide information, answers, and product at exponentially increasing speed.

I can tell you from experience building my brand that being faster is one of the most valuable currencies you can offer. With design schools pumping out new graduates each year, it has become a very crowded space for our core business of graphic and web design services. Everyone has an uncle, cousin, former classmate or friend who is a designer. The problem with graphic designers is they are notoriously poor at responding. I've heard countless clients tell me that they constantly wait weeks or even months to hear back from their designers, or get simple updates made to their websites.

My firm solves that problem and has become successful by having industry-leading turnaround times. Most projects are drafted by our artists and delivered electronically within 24 hours of receipt. This is a nearly unheard of practice, but we have become known for it and my team takes pride in it. We are heroes to new clients and valuable partners to existing clients and we have no fear of competition, because we have spoiled them for anyone else. In that way we monopolized speed.

Our second largest revenue stream is printing. If you've ever had the pleasure of walking into your local print shop, only to be told your job was delayed or misprinted I can feel your pain. That's why I decided I would only use local vendors that gave me the fastest turnaround times. My company, in turn, passes along that efficient service to our clients. We deliver their printing straight to their door, and in many cases, as quickly as that same day. Larger jobs might take 2 or 3 days, whereas my competitors take weeks. It's a differentiator that is tough to beat, and my clients don't mind paying a few dollars extra to get that.

Our profits have doubled year over year for the past four years mostly due to the fact that we are quicker. Notice I didn't say better (though I truly believe we are). It's my belief that being better in today's world is second to being quicker and more responsive. If you don't believe me, ask Apple's iPhone team. They built the best phone. It was better than all the rest, and they were top dog. Five years removed from building the best phone, their sales lag Samsung's. They didn't keep pace, so their market share got swallowed up by a hungry, faster beast. What they had was better, but they weren't quick enough to stay better. The point is, it's great to be the best, but don't expect to sit back and relax once you're on top. You had better keep setting the pace.

Some Tips for Getting Faster:

- Invest in a CRM or Project Management Software and use it religiously.

- Find vendors you can rely on who won't slow you down and will limit errors.

- Think 3 months ahead for promotions, sales and events.

- Incentivize your staff and reward quickness (without compromising quality).

- Cheaper solutions are usually just that—cheap. I've found cheaper to coincide with slower.

- Systemize your process and workflow.

- Write down instructions for tasks as they are created so staff has a set of clear steps to follow.

Today's brands must not only be faster in their delivery of service, but in delivery of relevant and useful information. Consumers connect with brands that open their warehouses of knowledge and ideas.

Often, brands are fearful to share their intellectual property. They think that by doing so, there will be no reason for customers to use their products or services. In reality, it's just the opposite. Sure, there are do-it-yourselfers out there, but the vast majority of people want on-demand service without any of the work. And trust me, you wouldn't want to do business with the do-it-yourselfers anyhow. They're often the ones that nickel and dime you, second guess your processes and are quickest to complain.

Take restaurants for example. It's nice to know the secret ingredients of your favorite restaurant's recipes, but cooking is time consuming and such a mess. I think most people will agree it's a lot easier to have a trained chef prepare it for you, along with a competent staff that will clean up when you've finished eating. Knowing how intricate the recipe is, and the exotic ingredients they used, makes us appreciate the meal that much more. But that doesn't necessarily mean we want to cook it every time we're craving it. And even when we try, it never looks or tastes quite the same, does it?

Along with this new speed of information another phenomenon has occurred. We now live in the age of the savvy shopper. With endless information freely available online about your product or service, managing your reputation can be a full time task. In fact, online brand reputation firms have begun to spring up everywhere.

Clients have expectations and preconceptions of you and your business before they pick up the phone, fill out a contact form, or buy your product. They know just about everything there is to know about you. They have read reviews, talked to friends and they have done their research. This puts brands in an interesting position which can be to their advantage or to their detriment.

An AOL / InsightsNow 2014 study found that "For 54% of planned purchases and 50% of impulse purchases, buyers knew the brand they would buy before they shopped." The study, aptly named "Buying at Speed", found "always-on shopping creates preferences that carry over into the active shopping period. While in-market targeting is important, brands must also consider having consistent ad/brand pressure to ensure that once an individual enters the active shopping window, they'll convert."

To put it plainly, the majority of consumers make up their minds in advance. It's your job to make sure there is a wealth of information out there in front of them in the form of press, advertisements, facts, figures, studies, FAQs, testimonials and the like.

Your Brand Must Take a Service-Centric Approach to Compete in the On-Demand World

In addition to research, customers are also demanding better service from brands. I recently attended a conference where the speaker asked the audience for a show of hands if they were more savvy and demanding now than they were five years ago. Just about everyone in attendance raised their hand. I'll wager you are a tougher nut to crack these days as well. And, guess what? Five years from now you'll be that much more difficult to please.

It used to be that you could get by just being the best. Those days are gone. You not only have to have the best product or service, you have to have the best customer service experience. Consumers aren't judging your service in relation to your direct competition; they're judging you by the likes of Mercedes, Bose, Disney and other exceptional brands they come into contact with. Those are the expectations you have to live up to when dealing with the on-demand buyer.

Tips for Successfully Feeding the Information Age Appetite

Most likely, you have a wealth of information you can share that's right under your fingertips. Here are some things you should do:

- Post daily messages across the major social networks

- Start a blog or knowledge base and post articles weekly or monthly

- Write a press release and share it on the major PR sites

- Post your PowerPoint presentations on slideshare.com

- Host teleconferences and webinars over Google Hangouts

- Live Tweet over Twitter to engage and answer customer questions

- Create informative videos and post those to YouTube and Vimeo

- Create a newsletter or whitepaper and send via email as well as post to online magazine sites like issuu.com

That's the Power of Free

Supplying valuable information for free can be a powerful way to maximize your brand's exposure. Valuable is the key word here. As I'm writing this, there are currently 2 million blog posts written each day. There are 144 billion email messages sent each day (of which nearly 70% are spam by the way). There are 175 million tweets sent each day. There are 40 million photos taken on Instagram. And there are 133 million hours of video watched on YouTube alone.[1] With all this and much more going on, it's increasingly harder for your brand's message to get through. The fact is, a very large portion of this information is garbage.

Content Marketing has become a buzzword in recent years and has quickly become a must-use internet marketing method because it offers a direct bridge between customer and brand. Content Marketing is simply providing information or images such as blog posts, infographics, memes, etc. in hopes of drawing the search engine spiders—and ultimately the consumer—to your site where you can then sell them your product or service. The problem is, most brands don't know how to harness it properly. They have a proverbial bridge to nowhere. In most cases, they are concerned only with the endgame - the sale. They have forgotten, or never taken the time to learn, the most sustainable means to that end- the loyal repeat customer

---

1 Source - Sean Valant, Hostgator.com

who is captured by solid gold content and valuable information that can stand the test of time.

Brands that supply new research or insights, provide useful tips, teach lessons through inspirational stories, or communicate relevant news create more loyal customers and brand champions. Brands that stuff keywords into blog posts, tweet about whatever is trending, or send out memes about current events unrelated to their brand or brand story, get what they deserve: fans and followers with no loyalty who come and go and do nothing for their bottom line. They are just useless stats on an analytics report.

It's important to make sure your communication and service continues to meet expectations. Once you've begun the process of creating great content, it's all too easy to sit back and wait for results. Fight through it, and pick up your pace. Remember, you'll need to be 200% as efficient in your delivery in a few years time. Once you've over delivered or gone above and beyond with your service, it's easy to assume customers will remember that and cut you some slack the next time around. That couldn't be further from the truth! In fact, they'll come to expect and even demand it of you. It's hard to swallow, but what you created or did for them yesterday doesn't matter. There are no plateaus in the on-demand world for brands that want to succeed.

Tweet the Deets:
There are no plateaus in the on-demand world for brands that want to succeed. #MovingTargets

Interview with Dave Hendricks, President of LiveIntent

LiveIntent is a New York City based email advertising technology firm that is redefining the way brands and publishers advertise in email. They are literally the Holy Grail of targeted advertising technology, which is evidenced by their client list, boasting the likes of AT&T, Disney, Mercedes, Bayer, Hyatt and other global brands.

Their proprietary technology allows advertisers to serve real-time ads catered to a consumer's targeted geolocation, time of day and other factors, alongside requested content from premium, third party email publishers.

In a nutshell, it works something like this: Imagine you own a regional restaurant chain and you have a special menu for breakfast, lunch and dinner. Using the LiveIntent platform, you can run ads highlighting your specials across the LiveIntent exchange, which is made up of the thousands of different email newsletters covering all sorts of subjects and services.

Now, when people within a 10-mile radius of any of your restaurants open any of these emails in the morning, they see something relating to breakfast. A few hours later, an email opener would see something geared toward lunch, and likewise before dinner.

Pretty cool, right? Add another layer, and that's where the fun really begins!

Layering in some third-party data, it can be determined that 10% are into fitness, so they should be served an advertisement with a healthier option. Or you could specifically target customers who've signed up for your restaurant chain's email list with discounts for being such loyal customers. That's the sort of targeting that makes for one dynamic ad campaign!

LiveIntent's website proudly boasts, "We're bringin' sexy back to email." I had the opportunity to ask their president, Dave Hendricks, how they're doing that and his thoughts on branding in today's on-demand world.

Gabe: The speed of communication and the delivery of marketing messages has grown exponentially since the birth of the Internet. Your company is on the forefront of that targeted / timely advertising. Tell me about it.

Dave: Email has always been one of the cornerstones of everyone's internet experience. It's one of the first things you get when you first get online. And when you get a new computer or phone, it is one of services that you set up as part of the un-boxing process. If you start working at a new company it is the one thing that signifies that you are an employee. Email is the original social network, almost a public utility. Like electricity, no one owns email but we all use it to one extent or another.

Your email address is your unique online identity, like your passport or social security card. You likely have several email addresses, often at least one for personal mail and another for work. Most people segregate their online activities between these two accounts, for example using the personal email for purchases and the work email for, well, work. This email address is the primary key that is used by retailers and other marketers when they manage your record in their databases. It is also the same thing they use to send mail to you. So the email address is a very durable piece of data.

LiveIntent doesn't send any email, at least like you would expect an email marketing company to do. LiveIntent works with publishers and brands that send email. We provide our client partners with an ability to acquire, reach, monetize and delight their email subscribers through our real time ad technology stack.

What does that mean? If a brand wants to acquire new subscribers, we provide them with the ability to place ads within newsletters sent by publishers to the publishers' subscribers, for example place an ad for their service in a newsletter sent by the *New York Times*. Before LiveIntent, there was no marketplace for buying and selling ads in third party media. We created that market, and in ad tech speak this is referred to as 'Programmatic'.

One of the most timely innovations that we have introduced is what we call 'LiveAudience'. LiveAudience employs a technique called 'CRM

ReTargeting', meaning we enable brands to use their CRM data – email addresses – to find their subscribers/buyers/customers reading newsletters sent by other publishers. 'LiveAudience' is a response to the problem of low email newsletter open rates. Most newsletters are successful despite the fact that often fewer than 20% of their intended recipients ever open them. What are the other 80% doing? Reading other newsletters, spending time on Facebook, Twitter, etc. LiveAudience enables brands to upload their segment data to LiveIntent, set a bid and then place an ad in front of a known customer when that customer is reading a third party newsletter. It's based on a real-time recognition of the customer based on email address hash-matching. Facebook, Twitter and Salesforce – among others – are now offering similar services based on the application of this hashed identification data.

LiveIntent also has built an exchange of email newsletters – it consists of hundreds of publishers and thousands of newsletters. The exchange is enabled by LiveIntent LiveTags – HTML code that lives persistently in the email templates managed by the publishers who are members of our exchange. When a user opens up an email sent by these publishers, the tag communicates with a LiveIntent server and at that time the LiveIntent service runs an auction and decides what ad to show each individual user. Through this exchange, LiveIntent is providing a new revenue stream to hundreds of publishers who could not efficiently sell the space in their email newsletters, alerts and notifications.

Some publisher partners of LiveIntent do not want to run third party ads from our brand partners, so for these publishers we offer the ability for them to optimize their own ads to their own subscribers. We call this 'Delighting the Customer'.

So we are using a well-understood technology (email), an accepted unique identifier (email address) and some new approaches (programmatic) to craft something that is going to be a game changer: CRM-based Marketing - wherever people are paying attention.

Gabe: What is your idea of the future of marketing at light speed over the Internet? What's the next big thing as you see it? Something new or an improvement on current technology?

Dave: When I think of the future there is a lot of 'right now' embedded in it, because we are seeing big increases in mobile adoption. When we first started offering our email newsletter monetization service in 2010, about 10% of the traffic that we saw was 'mobile', meaning people opening newsletters on iPhones, Androids and tablets. In the four years since then, the number of people buying tablets and using smartphones has exploded, resulting in about 50% of LiveIntent's traffic coming from mobile.

Identity is the other major secular trend. The experience of using the web as a logged in person is so much better than as an anonymous person that I will easily hand over the currency of my email address in exchange for more access. When you couple those two things together - mobile and identity - you get to the heart of why email is so successful now, and why it will continue to be.

Gabe: In what ways has the user or consumer behavior affected how you deliver your product or content?

Dave: LiveIntent's entire experience is dictated by consumer decisions: where, when and on what device they open email. What services they have subscribed to, what links they click on. As a system built on machine-learning, LiveIntent learns from what people do in order to deliver a better experience for them in the future.

Gabe: How has the on-demand consumer (the immediate gratification crowd) shaped the digital marketing world?

Dave: We have rapidly evolved from an era where latency - the amount of time between when a marketing message was shown to someone and when they acted - was measured in days and weeks to an era that has been ushered in by the always-connected individual who can immediately react or take action based on what they see in the palm of their hand. In a way, our devices have trained us to have hair-triggers. It's the ability to react quickly, rather than necessarily the desire, to which could be driving the instant gratification society that we have created for ourselves.

Gabe: Brands who don't feed the need of the on-demand consumer are destined to fail. Tell me more about the importance of timely marketing or brand messaging and placement.

Dave: Marketing messages are and have always been about content AND context. Smart brands don't rely on just-in-time audiences to create loyalty. Yes, there are some appetites that need to be fed, but smart brands have long realized that a mix of branding messages (not requiring a reaction) and direct response (driving a transaction) is a great long term strategy. Of course an ad for a portable generator right before a hurricane is always going to succeed.

Gabe: What signals / metrics are you using to put the right advertisers message in front of the right audience?

Dave: LiveIntent uses about 37 different signal types to decide which ad to put in front of what customer. Those signal types include, but aren't limited to: time, location, device, operating system, newsletter they are reading, membership in a CRM segment, gender, age, household income, occupation, size of company, previous effectiveness of an ad with someone similar, interest category and so on. This is all determined in real time.

Gabe: What new products or ideas is LiveIntent developing?

Dave: LiveIntent is working on bridging the gap between what you see on an email and what you see when you click in to an app or a website. Your identity should flow with you when appropriate. Harnessing technologies to make ads and content more relevant to you based on your identity is a big part of everything we build.

Gabe: You have a wide-moat, you have relatively no competition, how long is something like that sustainable?

Dave: If we keep innovating and doing things before other people think about them or can build them we can keep a lead. If you stop innovating on behalf of the end customer - the human - and you stop delighting all of your partners and clients, your moat is never deep or wide enough.

CHAPTER 2

LET'S GET PERSONAL

"Don't let anybody kid you. It's all personal, every bit of business...they call it business. OK. But it's personal as hell." **-from *The Godfather***

'm not saying you should take ALL your business tips from gangsters in movies, but the above line is as true today as it was when Mario Puzo penned it, and perhaps even more applicable.

We live in an increasingly impersonal world. One only has to sit on a bench in any shopping mall and look around for five minutes to prove my point. Children, teenagers and adults that walk by aren't conversing, they're surfing. There's less and less conversation or debate at the food court tables, and many more heads bowed low squinting at a smartphone, tablet or personal gaming system. The only people trying to engage are the kiosk clerks, and they're generally dodged like lepers by grim-faced patrons shuffling to their next destination. That's not just life in your local shopping mall, that's life everywhere.

Often I wonder if people enjoy the moment anymore, or if they're just too busy trying to capture it for Facebook or Instagram. Waxing philosophically, I ask myself, "Are we really there if we're just snapping selfies and looking through a lens on a smartphone?" But that's another conversation altogether. The point is, we're shutting others out more.

Just the other day I walked into my local bagel shop for breakfast with my wife. It's known in our neighborhood as a family friendly spot, and there were families there that morning all right. The table to our left had a couple both reading books on their separate iPads, and the table to my right had a dad sipping his coffee and checking his mail while the kids pushed buttons furiously on their Nintendo DS systems. In the half hour that I was there, the couple didn't speak to each other one time, and the Dad only looked up twice to ask the kids a question, for which he received a one word answer each time.

Here's the good news: you can make this work to your advantage. Our impersonal world offers brands an amazing chance to capture these conversation-starved consumers. Your target market is literally craving a personal touch. They're getting it less and less from their family, friends and certainly the companies they deal with. By simply having a human being answer your phone instead of voice prompts from a computer, you can take a giant leap forward from your competition.

The famous radio broadcaster Arthur Godfrey knew that words could create a dynamically different response if they could be directed at *someone*, instead of at *everyone*. Godfrey had been working as radio announcer in Baltimore, Maryland when a severe car crash confined him to his home for a time. During those days he had little else to do than listen to the radio. He noticed that most radio talent would use sweeping generalities and spoke to no one in particular. Radio announcers and hosts of the day would start broadcasts with, "Hello out there in radioland," or "Good evening ladies and gentlemen." Godfrey concluded that a more personal approach would be much more effective.

Godfrey decided to use a simple phrase to start his broadcast. Each time he began his show he would ask his audience, "How are you?" By using the word "you" he was talking to someone directly, and listeners felt as if he was speaking to them, right there in their home. He amassed fans and followers because he spoke on their level.

The reaction that a brand can achieve by simply talking to their audience, instead of at them, in a personal way is compounded in today's on-demand and impersonal world. Where there is lack there is opportunity; seize it. That's what the best brands are doing today and it's the easiest and most cost-effective way to stand out from your competition.

Remember my Gmail story? They used a silly word, "Oops," for an error message. The way they used it wasn't silly at all, however. What Google did in that moment was make the mundane personal. What I thought of as just a cold piece of software had a layer of depth I wasn't expecting. It didn't set in right away. That's because it crept in the back door, past the logical side of my brain (like most good branding does). Today's strong brands are personal and target the emotional side of the brain. They find ways to communicate more intimately because that's what we lack. Google could have told me, "There was an error processing your request," with some code or number for reference. But they didn't, and that was genius.

CHAPTER 3

THE MODERN, SAVVY CUSTOMER

A few years back, I had a client who was developing a large residential community near Ocala, Florida. The development was alongside The Villages, a massive retirement community. It's one of those places where there are more golf carts on the road than cars, and the early bird special is on every restaurant's display board.

My client intended to capture the market of the younger families who worked in and around The Villages. He wanted to attract upper middle class families who wanted a luxury lifestyle at an affordable price. Because home prices had fallen dramatically after the bubble burst, he could offer younger families the option of owning a home for more affordable rates than what they were currently paying to rent apartments in the area. He had wonderful homes but they weren't selling fast enough, so they hired my firm to help with their advertising and marketing.

The developer had a good product with a unique selling proposition, but he made one glaring omission. I told him there were no design or marketing plans in the world that could solve his problem until he fixed it.

"What's that Gabe?" he asked.

"Every time I've called your sales office, I've spoken to a very pleasant elderly man."

"Yes, that's Charles. He's very nice, but what am I missing?"

"Why isn't there a nice younger person answering the phone?"

"Charles is our receptionist, I think he does a great job, and he's all we have right now."

"You're right, Charles does a fine job," I told him. "The problem with Charles is he sounds like my grandfather, a little frail and probably not the image you want to portray if you're catering to young families. All your ads request people call you to schedule an appointment to take a tour of your homes. That means the first personal interaction your potential customer is having with your brand is the opposite of the image you're trying to portray. Don't you think a bright, energetic and professional sounding younger person might help get more tours scheduled? "

"You're absolutely right," he said. "We've been getting a lot of calls but people aren't showing up for the tours."

"I'm not saying fire Charles by any means, but maybe there's something better suited for him at your company."

Subsequently, my client made the switch and more people showed up to view his homes. It was as simple as changing who picked up the phones.

I see this happen in many other ways. Business owners routinely hand me flimsy business cards or cheaply printed brochures filled with clipart and ugly fonts. I hear music while I'm on hold that sounds like I'm in an elevator in 1985. I walk into stores that want to be hip, but smell old and musty. I see ads that talk luxury but look and sound five and dime.

Today's Customer Judges your Brand by Every Interaction

Good brands control every sensation. They direct not only what their customer sees, but what they hear, smell, feel or taste. They don't leave this up to chance or the whims of their employees. It's all a carefully orchestrated experience that is tailored to a particular audience, and strives to leave that lasting sensation until the next time you come across them.

Take Abercrombie & Fitch, a clothing brand with teens as their target. Just walking past their store in a mall, you will smell the cologne and perfume wafting out, you'll hear the pop music playing as soon as you cross the threshold, and you'll always be greeted by a teenager or twenty-something right when you hit the rack. They control the customer experience right from the beginning.

But no one controls the experience or has thought out every angle more than the world's most popular tourist destination for families: Disney World, the masters of managing each and every detail. Did you know they hired a Vice President just to manage the parking lot experience? They know that it's the first and last point of contact with their consumer at the park, and they don't want families left with a bad taste in their mouth because they couldn't find their car at the end of a long day. So they name the rows by characters, rightly assuming the children will remember it even if the parents don't!

Did you know they use real gold leaf paint throughout the park and paint the horses on the carousel each day? That's because they want the park to look fresh for the children riding and for their employees (who they don't call employees, they call "Cast Members") to feel pride in their place of work! The list of what Disney does to manage every minute detail—right down to the stitching of the clothes at the hall of presidents—would take a book or feature film to describe, but suffice it to say they succeed because of it.[2]

What's important to remember is that every customer interaction should be treated like a first impression. Until your on-demand customer becomes a loyal follower, he's probably already forgotten what his last touch was, so you'd better wow him or her this time. Don't skimp and don't cut corners when it comes to the external touches your brand makes. From experience I can tell you that you'll pay a much bigger price in customer retention if you go cheap when it comes to customer outreach and service.

Exercise

Good writers know how to skillfully use imagery—the language of the five senses—to create a more powerful and vivid impression on readers. Similarly, good brands manage interactions with all the body's senses.

A realtor I know sometimes arranges to have a freshly-baked apple pie or tray of chocolate chip cookies fresh out of the oven when she shows a house—it not only smells great, it triggers positive associations and encourages the potential buyer to envision themselves baking delicious things in their new kitchen. How can your brand address these sensations?

• What Your Customers See

_____

_____

_____

---

2 A very good book has been written by Tom Connellan called, *Inside the Magic Kingdom*. It details many of the lengths Disney goes for the sake of the customer experience.

- What Your Customers Hear

_____

_____

_____

- What Your Customers Smell

_____

_____

_____

- What Your Customers Taste

_____

_____

_____

- What Your Customers Feel

_____

_____

_____

- What Emotional Response Do You Want Them To Have

_____

_____

_____

High Pressure Sales Are Dead

If your brand is intent on succeeding in today's marketplace, you had better drop the high pressure sales tactics—they just don't fly anymore. That's because consumers have become so savvy, by the time they come to your site or storefront, in most cases they have already equipped themselves with the knowledge they need to make an informed decision. By doing their homework they've stripped the logic out of the sales process. They are not the putty of the past, waiting to be molded by the strong arms of a super salesman. They've done their research and they know, for the most part, who you are.

Think of the stereotypical car salesman of yesteryear. Their strategy actually used to be effective. "How can I get you to drive out of here today in this car?" and similar sounding lines were regularly trotted out to apply pressure to the buyer. It's difficult to imagine such hackneyed material working on today's consumer, who has the Carfax report and knows the blue book price for every model on the lot.

Sales today should be thought of as a gentler push in the right direction. Remember, your brand is selling an emotion, not a product or service.

Recently I met with some prospective clients. We went through our discovery session and I showed them some examples of our work for previous clients. Throughout the showcase, they were nodding their head and telling me, "Oh, I did like that one," or "yes, I remember seeing that one." It was obvious (and slightly flattering I must say) they had seen and studied my firm's work.

At the end of our meeting, as they got up to leave, they told me how they had found my company. It was a postcard marketing piece they had received over six months ago! They had been in the process of forming the business during that time. Meanwhile, they had been scouting out all types of agencies.

The wonderful thing about the research they had conducted was that I didn't have to sell a thing other than the expectation that I would be reliable and efficient. They knew the price, the product, the quality and the competition. In fact, their only real question was how long the design process of their logo and website would take! The classic question, I might add, for the on-demand crowd.

CHAPTER 4

CREATING AN EMOTIONAL CONNECTION

Modern brand building requires forging strong emotional connections with potential customers and clients. Today's customer, while savvier than ever before, still makes the majority of their purchasing decisions from the emotional brain. Although many pride themselves on making logic-based decisions, in reality there are very few consumers that buy for logical reasons.

Think about the last car you bought. You probably didn't buy it because it had more square inches of metal and leather per dollar spent than its competitor. That's what the logical brain would do. Most likely, you bought it for its appearance, the status it brings, or because it has a particular feature set you require.

How about the last pair of shoes you bought. Did you buy them because of the foam density per square millimeter? You were probably more concerned with the colors, the feel on your feet and the activity they were designed for. You may have even bought them because a professional athlete or celebrity you admire wears them.

In the industrial age, people bought for vastly different reasons than they do in the information age. Many brands are still trying to sell to the logical brain, though. Brands that understand the emotional aspect and how to connect on that level stand a better chance to succeed and crush the competition.

To find out what the essential ingredients to emotional connection were, I spoke with psychologists and behavioral therapists. In doing so, I found that much of what creates a buying decision in today's world translates into other areas like team building, negotiations with vendors or loan officers, partnerships, and other business relationships. Below are some suggestions that will help you forge deeper emotional connections for yourself and your brand.

Understanding / Empathy

The experts I spoke with agreed that the single most effective way to build an emotional bond is to have sincere empathy. This involves putting yourself in the shoes of your customer and looking at the world through the lens of their experience and struggles.

In the world of brand development, that begins with taking the focus off of you and putting it on the customer. It should never be about your wants and needs, but about your customers'. Great brands solve problems for their customers in profound ways because they understand the pain points and anticipate needs based on that understanding. Bad brands think their own problems must be the plight of the masses and create products that no one buys. They scratch their heads thinking, "What the hell is wrong with everyone? Why don't they get it?" What they lack is external clarity.

Great brands have external clarity. They are able to disseminate information and concepts in a way that their target customer understands. They are able to speak in plain English about complex ideas and leave the jargon for internal communication only.

Listening

Listening takes practice. Our human nature is self serving, so it takes a fundamental shift in thinking to truly open our own ears. Oftentimes we need to listen to what's going on beyond the words and read between the lines. That's a learned trait.

It's easy to hear what we want to hear. We do it all the time. How many times have you been disappointed by a meal or the service at a restaurant and when the wait staff comes to ask you how everything is, you politely nod and tell them, "It's fine" ? Most waiters and waitresses take that at face value and walk away satisfied. They assumed it was good and they got the answer they were expecting. Or did they? Fine is, in fact, not good. They heard what they wanted to hear.

The truth is, most folks are not so blunt and are too polite to tell you what irks them right off the bat. Very few servers ask a follow up question like, "Is there anything that would make your meal more enjoyable?" If they did, they might've gotten a totally different response like, "Well the salad dressing was a little salty," or "the bread was a bit stale." If they would have asked the second question they would have been able to correct the mistake for the next guests.

Another exercise in listening involves never interrupting your buyer or prospect. Again, because we hear what we want to hear, we often don't even know we are doing it.

I know a sales consultant that goes along on sales calls and records the conversations between salespeople and prospective buyers. After the call he will ask how it went and if they ever interrupted the client. The answer is almost always "no." He'll play back the recording and find out it is almost always yes.

Another tip is that whether you think the prospective or existing customer is right or wrong, it's important to hear them out, validate their opinion and never argue. Arguing with someone's opinion is an exercise in futility anyway. Opinions are just that, and who are you to tell someone that theirs isn't right? If your brand ever wants to lose customers, arguing with opinions is a surefire way to get you there the fastest.

It took me years to learn that silence can be a powerful sales tool. In the past, I've literally talked my way out of sales because I couldn't keep my own mouth shut. I would keep rambling on about the benefits of my service when my prospect was on the edge. Many times prospects need to digest the information you present. In sales, I've found that less is often more. Don't be afraid of pauses because they happen when people are on the verge of a shift or a big decision.

Experts tell me that summarizing or clarifying is an important way to show that you are actively listening and understanding. It's wise to sum things up and make sure you are on the same page. It shows you care about what you are hearing.

Lastly, make sure to ask related questions that delve deeper into their wants and needs, their hesitations or their expectations. Like clarification, these follow ups instill a sense of care and empathy.

Tune In to Needs

Deeper emotional connection is highly correlated with needs analysis and solutions. Many times, your customer doesn't know what their needs are; they just know there's a problem. You will know you are in-tune when you can figure out what they are lacking or missing without them spelling it out for you. Your brand will be the hero when you figure it out before they do.

Customers often have multiple needs, so dig deeper to find out what the priorities are. You may find that addressing the top need solves the minor ones.

Surveys are a great way to find out the needs and priorities of your target customer. I would suggest regularly polling your customers and asking a few short questions quarterly. Going further, I'd suggest you keep the questions open-ended rather than trying to steer them in one particular direction or another. By keeping your questions open-ended you have limitless possibilities for the ways they get answered. That translates to deeper realizations and needs you may have never thought about.

Here is an Example of a Brief Survey I've Used in My Service-Based Business:

- What are the top 3 challenges you faced last year?

- Where do you want to be this time next year?

- What is getting in the way of what you want?

- Where do you need the most support?

- If you could wave a magic wand, what would you like to see happen?

Those five short questions always yield interesting answers that I take back and brainstorm. When I come back with ideas and solutions to the needs found by carefully studying what's behind those answers, then I close more sales as a result.

Your employees have needs, too. Make sure you poll them quarterly at a minimum. Ask them what they like about their job, what they don't like, what they could use, etc.

A caveat to all this is to be careful not to make assumptions. Check with customers and staff to clarify their needs before you present your solution. If you don't, you risk seeming out of touch, or worse yet, offending them altogether.

Honesty / Openness

People are searching for brands that align with their ideals and values. Opening yourself and your brand up creates a strong emotional attachment. If you are passionate about a particular cause, express that in your marketing materials. If you've created a set of core values, tell your customers what they are so they can learn what makes your brand tick, as well as hold you accountable.

Being honest about your strengths and weaknesses also helps to attract the right prospects who anticipate the right results. You can't be everything to everyone, and today's savvy customer knows that too. The ones who do align with your vision, talent or unique selling proposition will appreciate it more and it will feel more exclusive. That exclusivity will forge a stronger connection. The ones who don't align just might tell a friend who does and could use your product or service. It will also save you a ton of time and headaches.

Making Them Feel Special by Acting Interested

When interacting in-person with new or potential customers, pretend you're dating. Think about what you do when you're on a first date. You put your best foot forward, go out of your way to show them what makes you unique and special, or take them to meaningful places. Above all else, on a first date you make it a point to be actively interested in the other person.

Another way to show interest is to pretend you're conducting a job interview or review. Ask follow up questions, praise accomplishments and recognize efforts. A word of caution: this technique does not work as well with wealthy or powerful people. They are used to receiving praise and accolades and are more guarded about opening up to this technique.

Having Shared Interests / Goals

Strong emotional connections are forged when your brand's goals and interests align with your customers. Having a tagline like, "We're passionate about seeing small business succeed," will obviously attract small business owners to your brand. Don't be afraid to spell it all out and put your cards on the table. Be clear about the ways you want to help your customers, and show them what you can do to help them attain their goals.

Charitable giving is an exceptional way brands attract similarly interested loyal followers. People are very passionate about the charities they give to. Often their lives, or the life of someone close to them, have been affected dramatically by disease or hardship that a particular charity serves. Charitable giving then becomes something very personal and dear to the heart. I've found that people who give to these causes will follow brands that align with their values with unwavering loyalty.

Warby Parker is a great example—they not only offer affordable and stylish frames that have made them the favorite spectacles of hipsters everywhere, they also donate a pair of glasses to someone in need for every single pair they sell. Their customers feel personally invested in the company's mission, and when they share their passion for the brand with their friends, that connection is obvious.

If your brand supports a charity, make sure it is highly visible somewhere on your website and other marketing material. Create press releases when your brand makes a sizable donation or contributes in a meaningful way.

In terms of shared interests, religious values probably garner the strongest emotional connection. If you don't mind your brand's target audience being strictly Christian, Muslim, Jewish, or some other faith that your company devoutly aligns with, make it known.

Compassion

In the world of branding, compassion is best portrayed by showing that your brand really and truly cares. Brands do that by providing value-added services or free advice. Consider writing special reports or white papers, or creating infographics that will help your customer learn and succeed. Don't make it just another sales pitch. Instead, do it out of a desire to see your customer succeed.

Here's a business-to-business practice that I use to show my clients I care about their success. My company regularly goes on review sites and gathers up all the good reviews that are left for our client's businesses and shares that with them. We show our clients how they can use those reviews as testimonials in their marketing videos, their website, their social media and more. There's no immediate sale or benefit to us, but our clients have a deep appreciation for us taking a piece of time out of our day every once in a while to do it.

Learning this emotional skill set and putting it into practice will build your customer base and make you more money. It will help you build a more cohesive workplace and foster growth amongst your employees. And it will get you bigger and better funding, and stronger partnerships and joint ventures.

CHAPTER 5

CORE VALUES - CREATING THE SEAMLESS EXPERIENCE

"A man got to have a code." -Omar, The Wire

Before you can truly master and refine the customer experience, it's best to get some housekeeping done first. The best brands have a team behind them that is cohesive, fosters internal growth, praises a job well done and is set up by their management to succeed. When properly implemented, this internal continuity transfers itself into the customer interaction and creates a seamless experience.

A major tenet of good branding is fostering an expectation that becomes a reality. When someone knows what to expect from your brand, they begin to trust your brand. Having a set of principles or core values sets your brand up to deliver on that expectation day in and day out.

> **Tweet the Deets:**
> Good brands foster an expectation that becomes a reality. #MovingTargets

The best way for a brand to develop these attributes in their employees is by instituting a set of core values that each team or staff member is held accountable to keep. I believe these values should reflect both internal and external vision. That is to say, they should encourage growth and a healthy work environment within a company, and also dictate how customers should be treated when coming into contact with a client or consumer of their products and services.

In no way should your core values be directed only to management or solely to lower tier employees. They shouldn't be made for only one division of the company that has to deal with customers. It's important that they are instituted company-wide and across the board. Remember, your brand starts from the inside out.

There is no better team working environment on earth than Google. We've all heard the stories of the ping pong tables, nap stations, relaxed environment, delicious free food, etc. What you may not know is that Google was set up in its infancy with a set of core values at its center. Google calls them its company philosophy, but it's essentially the same thing. You'll probably notice by reading them that they touch on a lot of the themes in this book. I've included the main points here, but Google actually spells them out in paragraph form in their document. I would highly recommend reading it. [3]

"We first wrote these "10 things" when Google was just a few years old. From time to time we revisit this list to see if it still holds true. We hope it does—and you can hold us to that."

- Focus on the user and all else will follow.

- It's best to do one thing really, really well.

- Fast is better than slow.

- Democracy on the web works.

- You don't need to be at your desk to need an answer.

- You can make money without doing evil.

- There's always more information out there.

- The need for information crosses all borders.

- You can be serious without a suit.

- Great just isn't good enough.

---

3 Google's core values can be found on their website at:

http://www.google.com/intl/US-en/about/company/philosophy

Below you will find my company's core values. I chose to keep our values short and sweet, but you can expound on your values, like Google, if you choose. Feel free to use the ones you like, toss out the ones you don't and add to what is here.

Shake Creative Produces Madison Avenue Quality Design on a Dale Mabry Budget efficiently and promptly, while offering world-class customer service.

1. Exceptional is the rule, not the exception.

2. We are professionals at the service of other professionals.

3. Mistakes will happen, but they should not be repeated.

4. The decisions we make creatively & financially have our client's best interest in mind.

5. Each team member is vital and valuable and is treated with respect.

6. We set emotions aside when we communicate with our clients.

7. If we see a need, we lend a hand.

8. We critique without being critical.

9. We are generous in our praise.

10. Each individual's attitude and work is a direct reflection of the team as a whole.

11. We don't know everything, but we can find the answer.

12. We never stop learning.

Once you have your core values in place they should be distributed to each and every person in the company, from administrative assistants to upper management.

I want to make it clear that every company, no matter what size or for how long they have been doing business, can benefit from having its own set of core values. If, right now, you are a sole proprietor or a company of two or three team members, please don't think this is something only bigger companies need and that you can gloss over it. It's even more important now to build that foundation for yourself, or within your small team. If you're a one person company, it will help your decision making, how you deal with clients, overcome hurdles and lay the groundwork for leadership if you plan to expand one day. If you have a micro-team it will lay a strong foundation of how your company can continue to grow, adapt and save its soul at the same time. If you have a business, big or small, that has been operating for years or decades without these values, you will find this can get you back on track—or keep you heading in the right direction.

I should mention that it's not enough to merely have these core values in place; you must hold yourself and your brand accountable to their adherence. I would strongly suggest you place these values on your website. On a regular basis—whether it's monthly, quarterly, annually or whatever makes sense for you—call up your customers or clients. Please don't email them, actually pick up the phone and call them. Remember, we live in an impersonal world. You can fix that for your clients. Talk to them and ask them if you and/or your staff have stuck to your brand's values. If you have vendors, I would recommend calling them too and asking the same questions. It's just as important to have happy vendors on your side as customers. A quick piece of advice: ask twice, or simply reiterate the question after you've heard the first answer. Often if you only ask someone once, you will get a canned answer because most people are inherently resistant to providing critical feedback. If they tell you that you have walked the walk, then treat yourself and your staff to something rewarding. If you haven't stuck to your principles, figure out where their pain points are and give your customers and vendors a definitive answer (not an excuse) as to how you will change that. Then, do it.

Lastly, I'll leave you with a story. A month or so after I instituted my company's core values and laid them out for my team I was faced with a challenge. A customer, who I had worked with since the infancy of my company, broke my rule #2 in a bad way. That rule states that, "We are professionals in the service of other professionals." For me and my staff, this rule is two-fold. We are to provide our clients with professional service at all times, and we expect to be treated as professionals in return.

This client had sent a very nasty email that bordered on a personal attack to one of my designers. The wording was disrespectful, the tone was condescending, and it was filled with all-caps and exclamation points that portrayed his disgust for a design she had presented him. He had done similar things in the past and I had swept them under the rug because I did not have a system of core values in place to address the problem. I had also been too scared to give up a client, fearing business would suffer if I did so.

My initial response was to start drafting an apology to the client. I was going to tell him that I would handle it and make sure we gave him something better next time...but I stopped halfway through, realizing this was the moment to practice what I preached. It was time to make a stand, get my employee's backside and show my entire staff I was on their side and my money was on the line. I responded to his email and copied the offended team member on the reply. I told that client that I did not appreciate his tone and if that was the way he was going to treat my team I would prefer not to do business with him. I left it up to him to decide if he would apologize or end our long standing agreement for monthly professional services. He chose the latter and we got rid of a cancer.

A few things came from that exchange. My staff respected the fact that I stood up for them, and held me in a much higher regard as a leader. I was their pit bull who would defend them at all costs, and that endeared me to them. For my business, it opened the door to a new client who we could now take on that paid twice as much and was ten times easier to work with. What a win-win!

Interview with Nick Friedman, Co-Founder of College Hunks Hauling Junk

So how does a brand create a seamless experience and retain its values when they are in a massive growth phase? I asked Nick Friedman, co-founder of College Hunks Hauling Junk, to tell me how. Nick and his business partner, Omar Solimon, took their weekend college gig, hauling away junk from people's homes, and turned it into a multi-million dollar business and national franchise.

Gabe: Moving is one of the most stressful events in someone's life, and the College Hunks brand is all about creating that stress-free environment for the client. How important is it for your brands to relieve the pain points for your customers, and what happens when you do that?

Nick: One of our focus areas as a company and as a brand is to provide a memorable customer service experience. Moving is actually number three next to death and divorce as the most stressful times in people's lives, so we have a great opportunity to provide people with a memorable experience. Ultimately they are going to talk about us, they are going to tell their neighbors about us and they are going to use our service again and become loyal brand angels—which is ultimately what you want to have happen as an entrepreneurial business. That's especially true in moving, which is highly competitive. So for us, we make it a real big part of our core competency to be a source of relief for our customers. As opposed to being an added source of stress, which tends to be the case most often when people are moving.

We get our employees to understand that, because what it boils down to is the experience that they provide. Everybody gets to empathize and understand what our customers are going through. It's not just about the moving day but it's also about when people buy or sell their home, or when their lease is up. Then they have to go through the process of applying for a mortgage, the process of showing the home, making a down payment, and all of that adds stress. If we can get our employees to understand where our customers are coming from, from an emotional stand point, it gives us a leg up to be able to empathize and help, and really, just brighten their day in one way or another.

Gabe: Your brand has a set of four core values. Why are core values so important to a brand, and how does it create a seamless experience for your customers?

Nick: When we first started, we didn't really understand the whole notion of what it means to have a company culture. We read a lot of books; we've gone to a lot of seminars by successful entrepreneurs and one of the recurring themes is that businesses which really withstand the test of time have core values that are actually lived, talked about, celebrated or rewarded. They were not just a set of ideals that are placed on the wall in the lobby and then never talked about or lived by the staff.

So we came up with four core values. Our core values are 1) always branding, 2) building leaders, 3) create a fun, enthusiastic team environment and 4) listen, fulfill and delight. So those are our four core values that we tell stories about in each and every one of our meetings. We reward and recognize our franchise owners and employees as individuals who have lived the core values and we use it as a litmus test for who we hire, who we don't hire, who we fire, who we let go, who we sell a franchise to, and who we decide NOT to sell a franchise to.

It really becomes sort of a guiding beacon for what the company stands for and allows us to attract people that identify with the core values. That is what creates the company culture—which creates the customer experience, which ultimately allows the business to thrive and endure the test of time.

They're extremely important, and the way we think of those core values is we actually did the exercises that Jim Collins recommends in his book. He calls it the Mission to Mars exercise. And he says, if you are going to send a handful of your best employees to Mars, and they are going to be observed by aliens and the aliens didn't speak our language, all they do is observe how your best employees conducted themselves—what are the characteristics, values or ideals that your best employees embody, that would be the reason why you would choose to send them to best represent your company? We did that little exercise several years ago, and that's how we developed our four core values. It's worked very well to create loyalty, from not only our team and franchise owners, but of course our customers as well.

Gabe: So when the customers interact with one of your employees, they get the same interaction when they are talking to anybody in the company, I take it.

Nick: Yes, well that's the goal—especially if it's a franchise organization. McDonalds doesn't make the best hamburger, they make the most consistent mediocre hamburger in the world. If you go to McDonalds in any city across the globe you are going to pretty much get the same hamburger and that's what people expect—what they get at one location is what they would get at another one. For us, our consistency of service, customer experience, and engagement with the client at the different touch points that we have is going to be consistent if we are to have a successful franchise brand.

Gabe: Your brand gives a very personal impression, evidenced in your design, the copy, the terminology you use and even your mascot. It seems homey, rather than slick. Why did you go this route and why did you stick to it?

Nick: Well, the name obviously is pretty catchy and when we first came up with it that was just that. It was sort of a name that just sizzled and stood out from a typical junk removal company, but the emotional reaction with the name and ultimately the experience that people had when they hired us—we saw that there was a strong emotional connection that the people identified with. They liked helping young people. They liked the notion of hardworking college students coming into their home or office to do this type of work and what it does is it elicits a level of trust in our brand, in our employees, in our company. Trust and care are two of the biggest emotions when it comes down to people moving or letting anybody come into your home, which is sort of your private domain.

We try to highlight or magnify those elements of our business and of our brand that people tend to gravitate most towards. So that's why we put so much focus on customer experience, customer service training and making sure we are delivering on that brand promise which, as you mentioned, is that stress-free moving or hauling experience.

Gabe: I've heard from a lot of different entrepreneurs and business owners that the consumer is just a harder nut to crack these days. Would you agree with that?

Nick: Yes I would. I think the consumer has been bombarded with even more marketing messages than they ever have been because now it's not just about TV, print and billboards, it's mobile advertising, it's all the news feeds and everything else. Not only are consumers overloaded with messages but they are also realizing that they can make much more informed buying decisions than previously.

Statistics will say that people's buying decisions are based on their emotion and then they will justify it or rationalize it after the fact with logic. Their first purchase may be based on emotion but then if they decide whether or not to come back, it's based on the experience that they had.

Now more than ever, you can research a company and its reviews. There is a sort of old school advertising approach to psychological advertising where they would coerce people into buying or elicit fear from people. Now, it's more of an educated consumer base. They can tap into their friends, their neighbors, their online reviews to make those decisions.

Gabe: Your brand makes a point to do a lot for the community and local charities. In what ways does that strengthen your brand and raise your profile?

Nick: I would consider us a value-based, purpose-driven business. That's something else that, when we studied successful entrepreneurs and business owners, is something that will allow any organization to withstand the test of time and the economic cycles - having a loyal employee and client base and ultimately a loyal community. Because when things do get tough it's not just about the bottom line or the revenue dollars that make the difference.

We've always been intent on being purpose-driven and engaged with the community, having support from the community that we service. We do get involved in a lot of charity, we do a lot of strategic partnerships with non-profit organizations like Goodwill where, instead of disposing or discarding the items we are hauling away, we're able to donate or recycle a significant amount of those items to get them back into the community.

Not only is it the right thing to do, it sort of fulfills our company purpose which is to move the world, and that's sort of a dual meaning. Obviously we are a moving company but we also want to move people emotionally; but it also has an immeasurable return on the business itself, where it creates a level of support that you can't tie into otherwise.

It opens doors through connection, through opportunities, and through media attention. It may not be the main goal of doing those charitable efforts to receive those results, but it happens as a by-product of it and we have seen it happen time and time again. It becomes a big snowball, then more good things get done and then more good things come back to benefit the business as a result of it.

Gabe: What are the ways you have found that work best to connect your brand to the modern day consumer?

Nick: Honestly, I think the biggest thing for us is through our employee engagement efforts. We have, at this point, over 500 employees nationwide that work for our franchise owners, so those are 500 potential brand advocates out there on a daily basis.

We have done some cool contests with our employees to help promote and encourage them. For example, we did a happy customer photo contest where they would take a photo with their iPhone or camera phones and submit it to our corporate office. It was a photo with the customer at the end of the job showing how happy the customer was.

That not only creates an employee that's motivated to try to make the customer happy but it also helps the customer feel good that they are contributing to this employee's efforts to be recognized by his organization at a higher level and it just creates more of that personal loyalty from the consumer. So I think engaging your front line staff in your brand mission ultimately helps them create that engagement with the community which ultimately again helps the business grow.

Gabe: Excellent! As you've grown you've added more service offerings like valet trash, portable storage units and professional organization to name a few. When a brand wants to start horizontally integrating, what should they be looking for, or what should they be mindful of?

Nick: It is very tempting to chase that next shiny thing because as entrepreneurs we are creative beings. We like to go after the next opportunity. So for us, the key is if it makes sense for our business, for our franchise owners, for our customers. And if it's something that we can easily do given our existing infrastructure, then we will move forward with that opportunity.

One service offering that we added when we first got into it is moving services. We had enough customers asking us to do moving, and we were turning them away for so long. Then we said "okay, let's try it" and we messed it up pretty badly. We were leaving bad brand impressions because we weren't experienced movers when we first tried to get into that realm and we had to consciously make that effort—we are going to be trucks and labor and haulers—before we could step into that space.

There is a saying that says you can't be everything to everybody, or you'll end being nothing to no one and I think that holds true. You don't want to be a mile wide and an inch deep with your service offering. You want to be recognized as an authority and an expert in your core service before you decide to add some auxiliary/ancillary services or products to help boost your top line growth.

Gabe: That's excellent advice! Lastly Nick, you literally wrote a book on working smarter not harder and having fun and it's aptly named *The Effortless Entrepreneur*. How can entrepreneurs build a fun, quirky brand for themselves?

Nick: Well, I think the most important part initially is to remember that you are starting a business to have fun. You are starting a business because you are not wanting to follow a traditional career path or you are passionate about this idea that you are launching into. If you keep that at the forefront, and as the key element of your culture and your values, you are not going to get away from that.

Obviously the notion of an effortless entrepreneur is a little bit of an oxymoron because there's certainly a lot of effort that goes into becoming successful at it. But I think what really it boils down to is the notion of flow. If you think of a pro athlete, a great artist or an entertainer when they are at their best and when they are at their peak performance, it appears to all onlookers to be effortless. When Tiger Woods was in his prime, his drives, his putts, his chips all looked effortless, even though he was putting in all kinds of work behind the scenes.

As entrepreneurs we were born with this ability to take a risk, to embrace change, to have a vision and to help lead others, but there are skills that have to go into that to allow you to become ultimately successful. So I think if somebody wants to have a fun, enjoyable business it has to start with what their goals are, what their vision is and what their values are. Then just pursue it and remember that it's a roller coaster. There are going to be down times and there are going to be up times. Look at it as your craft. The element of being an entrepreneur is your craft, just like an athlete or an artist or entertainer would look at their sport, canvas or musical instrument.

CHAPTER 6

COMPETING ON VALUE - NOT PRICE

can't deny it—I love the show *Extreme Couponing*. It's well done, entertaining, and a great look into the psyche of some obsessive compulsive individuals out there. My wife and I always find ourselves shocked and feeling somewhat cheated by the fact we are always paying full price. Then, we always talk about how we don't have all day to devote to clipping and searching for deals, or that time is money, and so on. In that way, we console ourselves, I guess.

With the emergence of Groupon and a slew of others, it seems we are quickly becoming a coupon-crazed society. I suppose it stands to reason, with unemployment so high, there must be more deal searching and time for that searching. But if you're like me, you see an economy like this as an opportunity, not a setback.

That's precisely why now, more than ever, I'm against coupons and all things deal-like. There's one simple reason for this: perceived value.

If you decide to discount your product, you are cheapening it in the eyes of the consumer. You are setting a dangerous context by which it will always be measured, even if only subconsciously. If a consumer can buy something for 50% off the "normal" price, at best they'll forever know they're not getting a deal at full price. At worst, they'll think of that product as not worth the price. That's not a good place to be, and it's a poor long-term strategy.

Why don't you see a Chanel product in Ross or Marshalls or another discount store? That's because Chanel is worth full price...at least to those who buy it. Those consumers are willing to buy it for that price because of its perceived value. It gives them confidence, pride, satisfaction and more.

Show your potential customer why they should buy your product. Make them want it. Make them yearn and strive for it. Make them want to show their friends they have it. Put that desire in their mind. I'm betting you'll gain a much more loyal customer that way.

Tweet the Deets:
When you discount your product, you cheapen it. You are setting a context by which it will always be measured. #MovingTargets

How to Avoid Competing on Price Alone

Great brands don't compete on price. Whether or not they are more expensive than their competition, people buy their products and services. Better yet, consumers make subsequent purchases of products and services from the brands they love and trust. If they can't immediately afford them, they'll save up or put it on credit. It's really an amazing phenomenon.

I help my clients shift from a reliance on price shoppers to a place where they acquire more loyal followers and brand champions. There are a few strategies of these brand transformations that I would like to share with you.

1. Be the Best

This is the hardest thing to do, so let's get it out of the way. You'll see as we progress that having the best product or service matters but it's not a game breaker if you can accomplish the others on this list.

Apple was the best when they released the iPhone. They had no competition because they created something more spectacular than anything currently on the market. It had a real internet browser, GPS mapping, a music player and phone all rolled into one. No other cellular device boasted such a toolset. They literally cornered the market and could charge pretty much whatever they pleased. That's a great place to be.

As copycats and further innovations from competitors came along their leg up diminished considerably, which is why relying solely on being the best is a dangerous game to play. You have to have a number of the intangibles that come next on this list.

2. Add Value

My car dealership gives free car washes. Yes, free. I couldn't believe it when the salesperson mentioned it to me *after* I had already purchased the car. My skepticism turned to endearment the first time I pulled up to the dealership with a muddy, bug-splattered sedan fresh from a road trip from central Florida. I handed the keys to their valet and 15 minutes later had a sparkling automobile pull back up.

This told me a couple things. Firstly, it wasn't part of the pitch; it was simply a value added service which showed me they cared. Secondly, their brand association was so important to them that they would prefer to have their cars looking as good as the day you pulled them off the lot.

When my wife was ready for a new vehicle, where do you think we went to purchase it? Brands that add value retain customers and generate repeat sales.

I would be remiss to not mention that when I looked back at what I just wrote above I realized I said "my" when referring to that dealership. That's how profound an impact something so thoughtful can make. If your customers talk about you in the same terms they would discuss their hometown football team—that's a great place to be (unless they live in Cleveland).

3. Give Something Away with Purchase

The make-up counters at Macy's and the world's department stores fill up on one or two special weekends each year. The ladies reading this already know I'm referring to the penultimate shopping event of the year: Gift. "We're on gift," those in the cosmetic industry say with a grin as they rake in the commissions.

As noted earlier, I'm strongly against coupons and discounts. I am, however, a big fan of "gift with purchase". It amazes me that a two-dollar tube of lipstick and a couple other nickel and dime items stuffed in a nylon bag would create such a buzz, but it never fails. Consumers will buy that $40 skin cream they could have bought elsewhere for $20.

4. Share What You Know

Consider sharing your knowledge in the form of a white paper, e-book or newsletter. You could also provide a seminar or workshop live or online. You have tips, tricks and ideas that will solve potential and existing client's problems. When you solve someone's problem, you create a life-long brand champion.

I know a CPA that hosted a seminar on the Affordable Healthcare Act for her clients. It's a seemingly unrelated subject to what she does as a bookkeeper and accounting firm, but it worked incredibly well. She brought in an expert who educated the audience on how this new system would operate and how it would translate to their finances. After the seminar she received dozens of referrals from her clients that were eager to tell their colleagues and friends what a wonderful accountant they had who knew everything there was to know about this new frontier. She became someone they trusted even more. When people trust a brand, they convince their friends for you.

5. Follow-Up

I'm a part of a business networking group here in Tampa that is a for-profit company. Each month they ask for my goals. Each month I get a postcard in the mail from them that re-iterate my goals. The first time I received that card I was floored. It showed that they were truly invested in my success, and that follow-up made all the difference when it came time for me to consider which professional associations and groups I would invest my money in (and more importantly, my time) the next year. Of course, they made the list. No, they weren't the least expensive association in which to belong, but their follow up was unmatched and it made an impact in the way I viewed them. I also refer other business owners to this group and have become a champion for their brand.

6. Don't Wait to Hear From Them—Reach Out

This tip will not only build brand champions, it will also alleviate a great number of customer service issues. Sales will come from this naturally if done sincerely, but will suffer if your messages are used solely as a sales tactic.

I switched to a new CRM for my business recently. A few days after registering my account, the software company emailed me some tutorials on how to better use the system. A few days after that, they emailed asking if I had any questions and where I should direct them. Every once in a while I'll get emails on ways to better use their system, more tutorials that might be of help and new product offerings. Those initiatives let me know they are dedicated to my success and they also get me more plugged in. The better I know how to use the system, the more I use it and it becomes part of my routine. When I outgrow my level of subscription, I'll be a lot less likely to shop around. I, like most, will stick with something I know how (and/or have the support) to use.

Reaching out can also prevent problems down the road. I have a client who regularly follows up with customer satisfaction surveys. On more than one occasion, they learned their customer was unhappy with the service. The customers had never made them aware, but had sworn to never buy from them again and to file a complaint. That all changed when they followed up. They were able to rectify the problems of the angry customers. They avoided a few BBB complaints that would have severely damaged the wonderful reputation they had built in the community. They turned those angry customers into happy ones because they took the time to reach out.

7. Provide a Useful Tool

This year we gave our clients a calendar of all the major events and holidays in 2014. We received a barrage of emails thanking us for it. Not only does it help our clients plan their events and marketing efforts, they think of us when they do!

Ikea provides a paper measuring tape when you shop at their store. I've seen realtors provide a mortgage calculator on their site. These are all great tools that customers appreciate and return to use, and it keeps you at the top of their minds.

8. Give Thoughtful Presents to Your Best Clients

My financial advisor gave me a nice pen one Christmas. Naturally, I started thinking of him every time I used it. Consequently, I made a lot of stock purchases that earned him commissions. I used him, even though I could have used a service like E-Trade for about a quarter of the price. That pen just endeared him to me. I wasn't shopping on price anymore; I was doing business with someone who cared.

9. Anticipate Their Needs

Great brands create desire by anticipating a need in the marketplace or in the eyes of their client. Most things we consider innovations started as anticipations. Tablets, remote ignitions, magic erasers and most every innovative product we use today started as anticipation.

An insurance rep I know reached out to me when he learned I was going to have a child. He anticipated I would have health insurance needs, life insurance needs, and more. Months after my son was born, he again rightly anticipated I would be thinking of beginning a college savings fund and presented me a unique insurance product I could use as a tax free savings fund. He got my business, and my respect, because he simply anticipated my needs.

10. Offer a Rewards System

This is something nearly every major retailer practices. Simply put, if I buy five ice cream cones from you and get my sixth free, I'll probably get my ice cream fix from your shop rather than the guy down the street, regardless if his ice cream is cheaper. There's a reason they are called customer loyalty programs.

11. Help Them and They'll Turn to You

I knew a manager of a business who was laid off. I knew she was great at what she did and felt it was an unfair decision. When I heard what happened I called her personal cell to express my sympathy and vowed to keep my eyes open for any positions that would be a good fit for her. About six months later an opportunity became available that I knew she would be perfect for. I put her in touch with the company and she was hired a couple of weeks later. That day I built a brand champion for life, and later on won a large new account where she is now employed. I didn't do it for that reason—but it exemplifies my point.

12. Be a Connector

You've got a contact sphere, so use it to your advantage. Last year one of my golf & country club clients was in need. They were doing a fundraising tournament but lacked a good way to promote the event in the community. They were also frustrated with the charity they had donated the proceeds to the prior year because they never showed up to support the event or even receive the check! I told them I would help, but I didn't have an answer at that moment.

When I got back to my office I was brainstorming ways to promote the event when I realized I was sitting on it the whole time. I had recently begun doing some design work for a non-profit that had some high profile celebrity connections. They could use the money, and the club could use the exposure. It was a perfect match, and I was able to endear myself to both companies because I simply put them in touch.

When you can connect your client to something they need or find them more business, you are much more than a vendor, you're a partner. Vendors come and go, but partners are life-long relationships.

CHAPTER 7

DEFINING YOUR TARGET AUDIENCE

"Who are you people?" –Patrick Star, SpongeBob Squarepants

K nowing exactly what you want your brand to stand for is the first step to developing your company's look, voice and perception. If you're a solopreneur, figuring this out will give you a direction and help you find the right partnerships and talent to surround yourself with to give you an edge over the competition. If you're a medium-to-large company it will give your personnel a solid foundation in which to create, live up to and outperform.

When inventing or reinventing a brand, there is a worksheet I go through with my clients. This helps kick-start the creative process and discover the deepest feelings and emotions we want the brand to portray.

This process is a simple but powerful way to craft the look and feel of the brand for us. I invite you to fill this out for yourself. I promise it will not only make you think, but will give you a new sense of direction for your brand. For some, there will be an "ah ha" moment, and you might discover something that you never thought of before.

This exercise is divided up between external and internal questions. Both are just as important as the other.

Part 1 - Defining your target Audience

1. Who is most likely to buy your product or service?

_____

_____

_____

2. What problems do these people face that you can solve?

_____

_____

_____

3. What are your secondary markets?

_____

_____

_____

4. How will you do it better for them?

_____

_____

_____

5. Who is your main competition (if any)?

_____

_____

_____

6. What is your competition missing out on?

_____

_____

_____

7. How much market share do you think you can grab?

_____

_____

_____

8. What brands do you admire and why?

_____

_____

_____

Part 2 - Internal

1. What 3 Adjectives or Feelings Do you want to Portray? (i.e. - Luxurious, Approachable, Peaceful, Powerful)

_____

_____

_____

2. What do you want to be known for?

_____

_____

_____

3. What makes you unique?

_____

_____

_____

4. What advertising mediums do you plan to use?

_____

_____

_____

5. What feeling or emotion do you want them to come away with?

_____

_____

_____

CHAPTER 8

STARTING A CONVERSATION

"How YOU doin'?" –*Joey, Friends*

The other day I was listening to Pandora in my office. Every hour or so a message pops up that asks me "Are You Still Listening?" Pandora pays music publishers for each song that is played. Naturally, they want to make sure you are listening, lest they pay for songs that no one hears. I totally get it, and I'm fine with that. I clicked the button and it went back to playing my music. After the third or fourth time I got a bigger bolder message and decided to actually read it. It said, "Are you still listening? We pay for the songs we play, so we try not to play to an empty room." It was such a condescending tone. It really rubbed me the wrong way. In my head I thought, you get paid for the ads I see on your site, so piss off! I decided to switch internet radio stations that day.

The on-demand consumer (in this case, me) doesn't care about what *you* want or what *your* problems are. They simply want what *they* came for.

Companies that brand themselves to the modern consumer, and who value the user experience, don't take that tone. They consider their words carefully. Here are a few ways I feel they could have worded it better, in a more conversational and down-to-earth tone, and kept me as a listener:

The "cool" approach would sound like, "The bossman says we gotta pay for these songs. Just tap that button below so we can tell him you're around and he gets off our back."

The "at your service" approach would sound something like, "We hope you're enjoying the music. Please let us know you're still listening by clicking the button."

The "buddy" approach might be, "Hey Gabe, Are you still around? Just checking. When you hit the button we'll crank the tunes back up for you."

The Problem with Submitting

We've seen that words and context are important to get right when dealing with today's consumer. However, nearly every internet form ends in a button that asks the user to "submit." What a horrible way to close the sale or opportunity! The word "submit" gives the connotation, whether consciously perceived or not, that the user should yield to authority. What a terrible thing to say to someone!

The button at the end of all the forms on my site reads, "Let's do this!" I chose that because I want to create excitement, passion and fun. My company is called Shake, after all. I suggest you choose the wording of your buttons, and other calls to action (printed or online) to suit the personality of your brand. Don't be afraid to break conventions. Make them as unique as your brand.

Changing Brand Speak

In any kind of written communication with customers, voice and tone are important, whether it's an email blast, direct mail or your website's "error" message. While marketers have long been aware of the difficulty of accurately conveying tone through the written word, thanks to the rise of texting and instant messaging, we are ALL now aware of the potential for miscommunication due to tone. Everyone has gotten a text from a friend that was meant to be friendly and innocuous, but something led us to believe otherwise—was that "FYI" supposed to be informative…or sarcastic? Even the simple (and grammatically correct) act of placing a period at the end of a text message can be interpreted as rudeness. Here are a few tips on defining and tailoring your tone and voice, and look at some all-too common tonal mistakes.

Don't Talk "At" Customers, Talk WITH Them

I had a friend in college who would talk AT me. He wouldn't react to what I said—he would just keep moving forward with his rant. Even WHILE I was talking, I could tell by his eyes that he wasn't listening to me, not really: he was just thinking of what he would say next. Instead of reacting to my words and having an organic back-and-forth, he would just be making a canned speech, essentially. Often his "responses" to my observations had nothing to do with anything I had said—they were just a direct continuation of what he'd said before.

Advertisers make this tonal mistake, too. It's a bit of a cliche, but don't talk AT people, talk WITH them. Customers want to feel you realize there is a real person on the other end of the screen/phone. All too often, brands take a boastful or condescending tone. When your brand's voice is smug and self-congratulatory, it's a turn-off.

Choose a Tone and Stick To It

So how do you settle on the proper tone? The last thing you want is to adopt some trendy, jive-talking flavor-of-the-month slang, especially if it has nothing to do with your product, company, or values. Sounds obvious, but first we must identify what's important to you in order to make a decision. So what is your company all about? What do you want your brand's "personality" to be? Remember the Core Values we covered earlier—now is when having those values clearly articulated will help you make decisions. At first, just try to boil things down to two or three keywords. A technical support company may want to convey that they are "dependable" or "knowledgeable." An organic smoothie hut might go with "purity," "honesty" or "nourishing." These words should be the primary factors informing and shaping your voice and tone.

It's also important to consider how formal or informal the tone will be. A more formal approach is direct and to the point--it uses correct grammar, spelling and punctuation, and minimal personal asides or jokes. This is used when you want to convey a sense of no-nonsense, hardworking professionalism. It works well with legal services, insurance, and with pharmaceuticals--in short, things people don't want to joke around about. It can also impart a sense of authority for high-end goods or luxury services.

An informal tone can ignore some grammar rules, crack jokes, and generally allows more creative freedom. When you need to come across as more friendly and likable, adopt a more informal tone. Brands that are specifically targeting Generation Y often take this approach.

Keep it totally consistent—remember the old saying, "familiarity breeds trust." The more familiar and consistently recognizable your voice is, the more your customers will trust you. ALL of your communications should have the same voice, and that means that all of your employees should have a thorough understanding of it. If your tone is inconsistent in different markets, or the voices of the print ads and the e-mail blasts aren't aligned, it will erode trust. However, it's OK not to have your tone fully nailed down right away--allow some wiggle room for your tone and voice to grow and evolve naturally.

Here's a simple exercise you can use to help pinpoint your values and tone. Imagine you could have ANY celebrity at all be your company's spokesperson. Who would it be? Why? Far from just daydreaming about possibilities, this can help you better identify what it is you're trying to achieve. Weight-Watchers has Jennifer Hudson, and she is a great match for what they are all about: she's an inspiring, motivating figure (she won an Oscar at age 25) while at the same time projecting youthfulness, and she embodies the goal of the company: she follows the plan, sticks to it, and we can see the results. She's a walking fulfillment of the company's promise to help people make better diet choices, and thereby improve their lives.

In 2009, AT&T created a TV spot for their new 3G laptop card. They distilled their message down to one core value: "speed" (specifically, the speed of an internet connection). To clearly forge a connection in the minds of the viewer between the product and the value, they used Floyd Mayweather, a boxer renowned for his hand speed. The connection being, he's lightning fast and so is their 3G laptop card. The speed of his fists and the speed of the internet connection are now entwined together in the mind of the viewer, and it was perfect.

Of course not everyone can afford a Jennifer Hudson or "Money" Mayweather, but that's not the point. Simply identifying who would be a good fit as a spokesman can help you refine what you want to say.

Humor as a Tool

Using humor in your daily interactions with clients can make their experience feel more personable. MailChimp, my favorite email marketing solutions, is a brand that has mastered this art. They've created a humorous brand personality that is reflected right down to the error messages on their forms. When you register for your account and choose a username that has already been taken you don't get a canned error like so many sites display.

Instead you get an amusing message informing you, "Another user with this username already exists. Maybe it's your evil twin. Spooky."

It's so much better than the robotic standard "This username has already been taken. Please select another one." It cushions the sting of not getting the name you wanted with a little bit of humor. By tweaking the tone, even an annoying development like a customer being unable to get their first pick of usernames can be deflected and turned into a positive interaction. It's funny, personable, and again, the language is talking with the client, not at them.

Another way MailChimp uses humor is with their mascot, Freddy the chimp. People love this smiling little guy--he pops up a lot when customers are using MailChimp's services to "help" them send emails and broadcasts. An endearing and judiciously used mascot isn't just for sports teams--it can strengthen brand identity greatly. But keep consistency in mind--do try to keep it to ONE mascot (we're looking at you, Geico--is it going to be the gecko, the stack of money with googly-eyes, or the cavemen? PICK ONE ALREADY!).

A Quick Word on Slang

Using slang can be an easy way to give your voice a dose of personality. However, there are pitfalls involved, one being that slang can make your copy feel out of touch or dated. If your target audience is mostly one age or geographical group, then you can use "their" language...but if you're attempting to reach a broader base, than niche-group slang can alienate potential customers. And be careful with teen slang, or whatever it is you *perceive* to be teen slang. Odds are, if it's reached the mainstream, the kids probably aren't saying it anymore. It's very easy to appear "fake" using slang--after all, this is the language of skaters and subcultures, not of corporate suits and boardrooms.

CHAPTER 9

SPEAKING YOUR CUSTOMER'S LANGUAGE

I'm a huge proponent of quality over quantity. The best ads and marketing pieces are brief, straight to the point, and each word is carefully crafted to elicit a reaction.

Too often ad requests come into my agency with little to no thought behind them. Believe it or not, these poorly developed campaigns come from multi-million dollar businesses and startups alike. In general, as in about 95% of our requests, these ads lack clarity, consistency and anything that resembles a well formulated plan.

I'd say there are two extremes to the spectrum. On the one hand there's those that just slap some verbiage together and expect us to extrapolate some deeper meaning from it and make their product or event a success. There might be a few random bullet points, contact info and an offer and the expectation is that we can figure the rest out. Then you've got the ones that give us pages of detailed information, company history, positioning statements, etc. and expect us to fit it all onto a quarter page ad.

We discussed earlier that we live in an on-demand world, and that means people aren't ready to read a 1,000 word missive unless they are truly entrenched in and fascinated by your brand. But you also don't want to sell yourself or your audience short by not providing the fundamentals that will get them to take the next step forward in your sales process, whatever that may be.

The ads that work do a few things well. Here are some tips I can offer, and I recommend you do them in this specific order:

1. Start with the endgame in mind. Decide what you want the action to be when someone has come across your ad. Do you want them to pick up the phone? Do you want them to go to your site? Do you want them to download your app? Figure out what one (importantly just one, not two or three or more, just one) thing you want them to do, and line up the rest of the pieces with that single clarity.

I can't stress enough that the call to action is the single most important part of the ad, and it's all too often a mixed message. You see phone numbers (sometimes two or three of them even!), fax lines, web addresses, QR codes, and all sorts of things all mixed up in one hodgepodge at the bottom. This is quite possibly the worst thing you can do. If you want them to call, provide one phone number and nothing else. If you want them to visit your website, provide it and leave out everything else. If you want them to scan your QR code, make that the focal point, not just something stuffed into the corner.

2. Design the words and look of the ad with your target in mind. Every company should have a clear picture of who their avatar is. They are your perfect client and the embodiment of your average customer. *Check out the sidebar to learn who my avatar is.*

A common mistake I see in ads is that there isn't a focus on the target. Companies try to be everything to everyone. Unless you're Coca-Cola, that simply doesn't work. You need to craft your marketing around a pinpoint targeted audience.

3. Think about where your ad or campaign will be placed before you make it. Ads and marketing are not a panacea. You can't just make an ad, splash it all over the place and expect to get results. The best ads are tailored to a specific audience and designed around the medium in which they are going to be used, or the place they will be seen. You may need to change the copy out or swap graphics depending on the demographics of the publication you're placing it in. BMW ads in an auto aficionado magazine like *Car and Driver* might highlight technical specs, while the ads they place in a men's style magazine like *GQ* might show off the car's sleek curves and stylish design.

4. Consider your words carefully. There are words that mean roughly the same thing, but the psychological impact or associations can be very different. For instance, I never use the word "cheap", I always say, "inexpensive". "Cheap" suggests qualities like flimsy, shoddy, and generally sub-par. Inexpensive, on the other hand, simply costs less, but does not imply a lack of value. When someone is going to spend their marketing money with me there is not a "cost", they are making an "investment". The implication of course being that there will be a return and they are not just blindly throwing their money at me. A "cost" is a pain in the ass, but an "investment" is a means to a future pleasure. I provide design and marketing "services" not "work". Who wants more work? Not me, but I'd certainly appreciate some service! So think about the words you choose wisely, and you will go a long way to winning more business.

5. In print ads and collateral, keep headlines to a seven word maximum. Just like billboards, headlines should be short, sweet and to the point. Flowery language and copy that is full of adjectives doesn't do the job. Think of your headline like a billboard that will capture people as they go through life at 80 miles an hour.

6. Ad copy should be no more than 1 paragraph. The meat of the ad should be closer to a 500 calorie portion than the all-you-can-eat variety.

7. Consider the colors and imagery of your ad. First and foremost, the colors you use should be true to your brand. Imagery should be consistent to the look of your brand. Most strong brands have a style guide that shows the fonts, colors, and graphic elements that should be maintained. Additionally, I'd recommend hiring a photographer over using stock images if at all possible. Find a photographer you like and stick with them because they can keep the consistency in the shots that will be critical to capturing your brand.

Following these tips, in this order will take your branding and advertising to a level where you can be recognized instantly by your avatar and will get purchases moving in the right direction.

WHO'S YOUR AVATAR?

For my company, Shake Creative, that's a busy general manager of a country club. He has two kids. He wakes up early, takes a five-minute shower and shave, gets his kids ready for school, and eats a piece of toast with his coffee as he's checking his email. He drives to work with the weight of the world on his shoulders. He thinks of all the decisions he will have to make that day. He gets to work and finds he has 50-100 emails, most of them emergencies. When he's done putting out the fires he has members of his staff of 10-15 that pop in and out of his office all morning. He probably doesn't have time for lunch and by the time he looks back at his computer screen, his inbox is full again. He wants to have more members, but finds it tough competing with the four other courses within 10 miles of his club. His members drop in and out, and the board or his corporate office is constantly setting higher goals. But there's no time to solve the membership problem because the day-to-day hurdles get in the way. He finishes his day writing up his reports and doing paperwork. He leaves his office at 7:30pm and takes his meal on the couch where he decompresses with a few episodes of his favorite sitcom. He reads his kids a book and puts them to bed. He looks over a few emails on his phone and decides he'll reply in the morning as he crawls into his sheets. He wakes up and does it all again the next day. That's my avatar. Who's yours?

The Rules Have Changed, and You Didn't Make Them

In a very short time there has been a fundamental shift in the way customers and consumers interact with brands. Only a few years ago, companies could get away with poor service or imposing their iron clad will with virtually no repercussions.

It used to be that the worst offenses might garner a reaction like, "I'm going to write a letter to that company!" Today those empty threats have been replaced by folks who will post a 20 page website or blog about how much a particular company "sucks." They'll start a message board where grievances will be aired to the masses. They'll tweet their 5,000+ followers about what a horrible brand experience they had. So there's simply no way around consistently delivering the best possible service to your customers and clients 100% of the time, lest you feel the wrath of the internet.

Let me give you one case-in-point. A friend of mine had a bad experience at a new burger joint. They had just opened up, everything was new and clean, and the burgers were pretty damn good—but he had an extremely negative customer service experience.

He didn't ask to see the manager. He walked straight home, sat down at his laptop and composed a withering Yelp review while he was still freshly mad about the incident. Then he systematically moved on to about a half dozen similar sites and social media outlets, spreading his message. By the time he was done, this new business's digital footprint had been covered in mud. Anyone researching the new restaurant online was now very likely to see at least one of his negative reviews and other attacks.

The fundamental ways companies conduct businesses must change too. I constantly see companies clinging to what I would classify as relics of business practices long since past. They fail to realize that the new breed of savvy customer makes the rules. Customers do their homework now, so you better make sure your grades are up to snuff.

Crowdsourcing is the scourge of true artists. Great designers, writers, photographers, developers and other professionals lose out to sites like eLance, oDesk, Fiverr and the like. These artists bemoan the problem but at the same time, often fail to recognize the cause: clients changed their behavior and collectively as the market made their own rules. While I am opposed to crowdsourcing for various reasons (including my belief that you get what you pay for) I also recognize that my model has to change in order to succeed. Sure, I could whine about it, but what good would that do? Instead, I offer value added benefits and perks to my clients that they can't find from a crowdsource. In turn, they stay loyal.

I've come across some prime examples of businesses that lose out because they refuse to adapt.

Recently, I had a discussion with a photographer about the possibility of teaming up to service some of my clients. He explained to me how he worked and did his billing. He told me that his very reasonable fees included two years of rights free usage for his images.

"Two years?" I said. "Why only two years? If I'm a client and paying you for the work now, why would I want to pay you again down the road?"

"That's the way the industry works," he told me. "Any good photographer is going to offer the same terms."

Well that's all fine and good I thought to myself, but I can think of five other photographers, just as talented as he, who don't have the same restrictions on usage. When you couple that with the fact that my clients could potentially be forced to remove photos from their sites, packaging and collateral when those 2 years are up (including the cost of my time to do that for them) or pay the piper, it just plain didn't seem fair.

He didn't get my referral. It wasn't because he wasn't a great photographer, it was because he didn't consider the marketplace's wants and needs.

A similar story is that of the stock photography giant, Getty Images. In the past, designers and agencies would receive Getty's catalog in the mail where they could see all the images that were for sale. They would pick the ones they want, mail in their order with payment and get the images delivered by post to their office in a few days. The photos were $500 and up each and that was perfectly fine, because they were the leader in that space and had crushed their competition.

Today you can go on a site like iStockPhoto.com or Fotolia.com and find a high resolution photo for about $10. Getty images wanted in on that game, and added their portfolio to the databases. They set their prices at about half of what they used to get. So now their images, priced at $200 or so sit right there next to similar quality photos that are about 5% of the price. Designers like me see a great image from Getty, then look at the price, and move on knowing there's something just as good a few clicks away for a lot less. That's a strategy with inherent flaws. It's a business not recognizing who its customer is and trying to get by on an ancient pricing model. They would have gotten my download and at least my ten bucks if they priced themselves where the customer dictated.

Getty images finally changed its business model in the spring of 2014. They made the ingenious decision to just give their photos away to use on the web—as long as they can be embedded. People were stealing them or getting screenshots from other sites anyway, so giving them away for blogs and companies to use throughout the web now allows them to track data (which they can then resell) and allows for ad placement on their images. This is the perfect response to what the market demanded, and offered them a new (yet risky) business model. My bet is that it will pay off.

Here's a final story on this subject of leftover practices. It's one I run into quite often in my industry, and I still scratch my head. Web design accounts for a large part of our business. Many times clients come to us because designers have hijacked their sites and they need someone to either rebuild it or save it. What the previous designers have done is sell web hosting to their clients, built the sites on their servers and then refused to allow access to the site. It's business as usual as long as the designer / client relationship stays intact, but when it goes south the sites are out of reach. The clients have paid for the work but don't have access to what they've paid for. It's really a travesty and a terrible way to do business. There's also no excuse for it, because hosting companies have now made it easy for resellers to host multiple accounts with unique logins and control panels for every client. In my opinion, it's simply not worth it to hold my clients hostage to demand they use my hosting. At the very least developers should offer clients their own unique login and complete access to what they've paid for.

Speak your customers' language and they will begin to follow you, become loyal and, most importantly, tell their friends. If you think you can get by doing things the way you used to, or if you think you can impose your will on your clients, you'll surely be in for a surprise.

CHAPTER 10

YOUR LOOK MATTERS - MANAGING THE MINUTIA

W e've touched on consistency as it pertains to the customer experience, your message and more but consistency in the look of your brand is where it all culminates. The big brands and particularly their logos have become iconic because they understood the true value of consistency. For most Americans, if I say "Shell Gasoline" you think of their bright yellow and red shell. If I say, "Target", you think of the red bullseye. If I say AT&T you think of their blue world. If I say Nike, you think of their swoosh. If I say Coca-Cola you think of their handwritten logo and particular shade of red. Symbols and colors become synonymous with the words. That's the power of consistent, well designed imagery.

Brands who do it well manage the smallest details, down to the texture or feel of the paper their business card is printed on. They reject print orders when their colors are not perfectly matched. They have a brand standards guide that dictates the fonts that should be used and a myriad of other minute details. Do you think they do it just to spend their bloated budgets? Surely not. They know that consistency is critical to providing an expectation. Expectation in turn leads to trust, and trust leads to quantum leaps in sales—and even more importantly, repeat business.

The Logo

A brand's outward projection of its image starts with the logo. A great logo is simple, memorable, and has external clarity. Paul Rand, the identity designer behind many of the world's most recognizable brands (IBM, ABC, UPS, and Westinghouse to name a few) stated, "The only mandate in logo design is that they be distinctive, memorable and clear." If we go back to the list I mentioned above, were there any super detailed symbols or fancy effects there? Were there any that weren't straight forward and to the point? Were there any that didn't seem clear? Of course not.

The most memorable sports team logos will back this up. Rarely is an iconic team logo cluttered or too busy visually—think of the simple white "G" on a green background with a thin yellow border of the Green bay Packers, the vivid orange wishbone-style "C" of the Chicago Bears, or the feathered wing attached to the spokes of a car wheel for Detroit's Red Wings—a clever design that conveys speed while giving a nod to the Motor City's history as an auto manufacturer at the same time.

Now more than ever, people are inundated with images. A safe estimate is that people see around 15,000 images per day, and it's a lot more for the Snapchat and Pinterest crowd, I can assure you. That's why being simple and clean should be at the forefront of your design choice.

What a Great Logo Does

The world is full of bad logos, but I would rather focus on the positives and tell you what a good one looks like and does for its brand.

Great logos can be drawn by an 8 year old from memory. When I say simple, that's how simple they should be. My favorite logo of all time is Target. It's not complex, it owns its identity. It's two circles, one color and has simple typeface to match. I would characterize it as a refined look, and definitely not pretentious—just clean and to the point.

Tweet the Deets:
A good logo can be drawn by an 8 year old,
from memory. #MovingTargets

Great logos don't rely on color to make a statement, but the right use of one or two colors accentuates its message. A logo should be able to stand alone in black and white and still look good. In fact, many designers will draft the initial designs in black and white, then color only once the mark is perfected.

You're probably aware there is a strong psychological link to color. Orange is a color of change and transformation so I like to use that for gyms. Blue causes a calming sensation in the mind, which is why nearly every hospital and insurance company uses it. Black (though not truly a color) is powerful and luxurious; think Mercedes Benz, Chanel, Gucci. Red is a color of attention and excitement, but what you may not know is that it's a lucky color for Chinese. If your target market has anything to do with China or the Chinese, do yourself a favor and go with red. If you want to explore more about the psychology behind choosing the right color for your brand check out the sidebar.

Great logos can be scaled down or up and still be recognizable. You'll know your logo is too complex if you shrink it down and can't make out all the subtleties you thought made it so cool. Logos have to be adaptable to a wide range of uses like embroidery or screen print (which can't handle complex designs and too many colors), on a billboard where it has to be noticed at 80 mph, on cards, stationery, pens, websites, social media icons, and a myriad of other places. Before you green-light a new logo make sure it's adaptable and imagine all the possibilities and potential uses.

Great logos portray your brand's personality. Brands come to be known as whimsical, serious, luxurious, fun, modern and more by their logo. For me, font choice goes the furthest to set the tone when it comes to displaying the brand's personality. The best advice I can give is to step outside yourself and your team and run your proposed logo by a focus group of friends, colleagues and peers who haven't seen it before. Don't ask this group if they like the logo or not, ask them to write down three adjectives they feel when they look at it right off the bat. That exercise should let you know if the logo is resonating for the right reasons.

Now this might shock you, but some of the best logos attached to the worst brands can seem ugly, and some of the worst logos seem beautiful when they are put in the context of an innovative or powerful brand (I think of Google here). Paul Rand claimed "It is only by association with a product, a service, a business, or a corporation that a logo takes on any real meaning. If a company is second rate, the logo will eventually be perceived as second rate. It is foolhardy to believe that a logo will do its job immediately, before an audience has been properly conditioned."

Paper Matters

I said earlier that good brands manage their interactions with all of the body's senses, and I meant ALL of them. The feel and texture of the paper that great brands use is given a lot of thought. If you want your brand to have a soft, homey feel you could use a silk. If you want a slick, modern response go for a satin. If you want the vintage, luxury feel, then linen is probably a solid choice. The fact is, good brands manage not only the look, but the feel of what they put in the hands of their consumer. Think about that when you are designing the packaging for your product, or the brochures and business cards you produce. Everytime you touch a consumer, whether that's through visual, aural, tactile or gustatory means, that process should be thought about in terms of what will best display your brand's identity.

Music Sets the Tone

The music inside your storefront or office building sets the emotional tone for both your staff and your customers. It would be perfectly acceptable to blare punk rock music in a store like Vans of the Wall or Journeys. That wouldn't go over so well in a Macy's though. That much is obvious.

Apparel

The way you and your employees dress is another way to portray your brand's identity. Just like music, some places can get away with a casual vibe. Others may have clients that expect professionalism and suits are the only option. If your brand requires uniforms to be worn, think about the color (use the color psychology tips in the sidebar) and style. Again, once you figure out who your avatar is, this stuff will come naturally. Dress for them, and you won't go wrong.

COLOR PSYCHOLOGY

Psychology of: Black

Technically, Black is the absence of color. Black can set a very strong tone. Most often, it's associated with authority, power, stability, strength and luxury. However, it can also elicit negative feelings like gloom, death and somberness. For me, this really depends on the other colors it's paired with. Black with gold and silver usually leans to the luxury side, while black with red will feel a little bit edgier.

Psychology of: White

Technically, white is made up of every color of the spectrum. White signifies purity and cleanliness for most people. It's the favored choice of brides and doctors the world over. Some other connotations include safety (think light at the end of the tunnel), neutrality and creativity. Thanks to Apple, it has become associated with tech as well.

Psychology of Color: Grey

Grey is most associated with the practical, timeless, middle-of-the-road, solid things in life. Too much grey leads to feeling mostly nothing; but a bit of grey will add that rock solid feeling to your product. Some shades of grey are associated with old age, death, taxes, depression or a lost sense of direction. Silver is an off-shoot of grey and often associated with giving a helping hand or strong character.

Psychology of Color: Red

Red is by far the most eye-catching color, as well as the color of energy. It's associated with movement and excitement. It's even known to increase heart rates in those surrounded by it. In short, it gets people psyched. Wearing red clothes will make you stand apart from the crowd. Red isn't a color you want to overuse, but just a touch of red in the right place can work wonders. Think of the classic red "power" tie with a navy blue suit and a white shirt. To the Chinese, red is the symbol of life and luck, and for this reason, it's the color worn by brides in China. It's closely tied to love and giving—Christmas, Valentine's Day, red roses, etc.

Psychology of Color: Blue

Most people's favorite color. After all, much of the world is blue (skies, seas). It's certainly a peaceful, calming color, but that isn't true with every shade of blue. Some shades (or simply too much blue) may send a chilly, uncaring message. Bedrooms are blue because it's a calm, restful color. Over time, blue has come to be associated with steadfastness, dependability, wisdom and loyalty—many public servants wear blue uniforms, including police. Blue rooms can enhance productivity because they create an atmosphere of calm and focus. Some studies have even demonstrated that weight lifters can lift more weight in a blue gym – in fact, nearly all sports are enhanced in blue surroundings (which may help to explain the home field advantage of a certain college football team in Idaho).

Psychology of Color: Green

Green is the color of nature, growth, peace, harmony, and—for Americans, at least—money. Like blue, it's a calming color that's very pleasing to the senses. Deep forest green is associated with masculinity and wealth. Hospitals sometimes use light green rooms because they're found to relax patients. Other associations are envy, good luck (think of leprechauns and four leaf clovers) generosity and fertility.

Psychology of Color: Yellow

The color of the sun, associated with laughter, happiness and good times. People surrounded by yellow feel optimistic and cheerful because it causes the brain to release more seratonin. Be cautious with yellow—if too intense, it can be associated with fire and studies show babies cry more in vivid-yellow rooms. It can boost our metabolisms and elicit creativity—which is why notepads and legal tablets are frequently yellow. Some hues of yellow are associated with cowardliness (hence the term "yellow-belly"); but the more golden shades communicate the promise of better times.

Psychology of Color: Orange

The most flamboyant of colors. It connotes good times, happiness, energy and warmth, and is also associated with ambition. It's the furthest color from calm that you can get. A very popular choice for athletic uniforms.

Psychology of Color: Purple

In the ancient world, purple was nearly the exclusive color of royalty, and to this day is associated with wealth, prosperity, and rich sophistication. This color can stimulate the mental activity employed in problem solving. However, overuse in a common setting can seem artificial or fake. Use purple most carefully and judiciously to impart an aura of mystery, wisdom, and respect. Interestingly, young adolescent girls are most likely to select some sort of shade of purple as their favorite color.

Psychology of Color: Brown

Friendship, stability, and reliability belong to the color brown. People are increasingly likely to select this as their favorite color. It's the color of the earth itself—what better to denote stability? Natural and organic products are usually swathed in brown—but beware if you're introducing a product/package in India, where it is associated with mourning the dead.

CHAPTER 11

7 MARKETING MISTAKES BRANDS MAKE

Below are the seven deadly sins for any brand. If your company can avoid these mistakes, you can gain a serious leg up on your competition.

Mistake 1: Not Knowing What One Customer is Worth

Often I come across a struggling brand and during our discovery session I'll ask the simple question, "So what's an average customer worth to you?" The response that comes out first is rarely the number we reach at the end of the discussion. Usually I'll get an answer that calculates the average purchase price. I deal mostly with country clubs so they'll generally add up the initiation fee and possibly include the monthly dues over the course of one year.

At this point I'll ask (in the case of a golf and country club) if the members occasionally take their meals at the club. Of course the answer is, "Yes." Then I'll go on to ask if they ever attend any of the clubs events and parties? Do they ever rent the events space for a party, wedding, or meeting? Do they bring guests and pay cart fees or tennis court fees? Do they ever purchase anything from the pro shop? Yes, yes, yes and yes.

Now we're getting somewhere. So now we've found that one customer, or in this case, member, is worth a whole lot more than their dues. Then I ask a question that even the sharpest of owners, GMs, and membership directors rarely account for. Do they ever refer their friends? At this point I've really got them thinking.

Until you have the numbers right on what a customer is actually worth, there's no point in trying to figure out how much you should spend on marketing to them. There's also no way to accurately gauge their impact on your bottom line, or to what means you should go to retain them.

Mistake #2: Forgetting to Keep Track of Marketing Results

Many brands aren't tracking their marketing results and don't know what is working and what is not. They are throwing advertising dollars around, and just hoping for something to work with no plan in place. How do they know where to put their money the next time? I assume they just must like gambling. I get answers like, "I think we got a few new customers from the last direct mail campaign we ran," or "I know we got some calls, but not sure where they heard about us." This is a dangerous game to play and one that is sure to close doors sooner than later. Make sure you track absolutely everything.

Mistake #3: Thinking Throwing Money Around Will Fix Things

This goes hand in hand with #2. Often, brands that aren't tracking what is working start throwing marketing money around when it's not. When customer numbers drop, they start to place ads in the newspaper, dump some funds into an AdWords account, or suddenly start sending out weekly email blasts. With no plan, or way to track, they think that new business will just start flowing in. Unfortunately, it just doesn't work that way. You need to define your niche, find where they are hiding, and speak to them in a tone they can relate to.

Mistake #4: Not Having a Great Loyalty Program or Re-Marketing Program

Loyalty programs do exactly what they say, keep customers loyal. It gives them a reason to keep coming back. I strongly recommend you find some ways to implement them in your marketing efforts.

Re-marketing programs directed at former customers often yield great results for little cost. My own business consultant told me on the first day we met that the easiest person to sell to is the one who just bought. It was true then, and still holds true today. Past customers are familiar with your brand, and barring any circumstances where you severely offended them, they probably would at least consider coming back if you asked nicely enough. They may have disappeared for reasons like temporary economic hardship. Quite possibly they are back to being flush and just forgot how much they enjoyed your product or service. Remind them.

Mistake #5: Not Defining & Speaking to that Audience

As we've seen, your brand can't be everything to everyone. That's a good thing, you can use it to your advantage if you play your cards right. Many brands have an identity crisis because their ads say one thing, and the prospective customer's expectation isn't met when they come pay a visit to their store or site.

Is your product geared to the 60+ aged demographic? It's almost useless to put all your marketing effort into social media to attract them. You'd be better served with a direct mail campaign. Simple things like that make all the difference.

Mistake #6: Failure to Follow Up With Their Needs & Wants

Brands could save a lot of customers if they would simply ask more questions. I hear team members asking all the right questions at all the wrong times. They ask them when it's too late, and the customers are leaving. I suggest you send out surveys or place them in store or on your site to continually take the pulse of your brand. Don't think a simple suggestion box will do the trick either. It takes more. Ask them what you can do to improve their experience. What types of innovations they would like to see. Ask them if your staff is treating them properly. Ask them tough questions. Even if you are uncomfortable with the answers you will be better equipped to fix the problems and capitalize on the wins. As an added benefit, you might even get some new product or service ideas from the feedback.

Mistake #7: Failing to Figure Out What the Competition Is Doing Better

It's easy to stand pat and live in a bubble. It takes some effort to find out what's working at the business down the street. If you're losing customers to your competition, figure out what they are doing better than you. Even if your brand has dynamite sales numbers, you should still find out what you can do better. It's arguably even more important during the good times because you can keep the momentum going and start really running laps ahead of the competition.

CHAPTER 12

BRANDING A LIFESTYLE

A s we've discussed, more and more brands are focusing on the emotional connection to the consumer and giving their product a personality. I can't think of anyone who has done this better (and in the midst of an economic downturn!) than Beats Audio. When they arrived on the scene in 2008, their brand positioning was in stark contrast to more mainstream offerings that were competing on the merits of sound quality or affordability. Beats headphones carry an average $300 price tag, and most audiophiles will tell you that their sound quality is on the lower end of subpar. All things equal, Beats shouldn't have had a shot in hell to capture market share. So why does every American teenager want a set of Beats headphones for their birthday? They branded a lifestyle, of course.

Beats decided to market their headphones as a lifestyle choice. Their target demographic was teenagers and Gen Y'ers. They partnered with Dr. Dre, the legendary hip hop star and producer. Beats headphones were designed to look modern and cool with their shiny black and red finish and sleek curves that would be a fashion statement, not just a piece of gear. They got famous musicians to represent the brand, like Alicia Keys. Their first ads featured Dre and other artists sitting in their homes and studios and telling the audience that they too could "Finally, hear music the way the artist intended." In essence, they were letting their target audience of teenagers and young adults know that they could finally connect to their heroes, hear what their icons heard and feel what the artists felt in the form of an audio product.

Their ads now feature famous athletes like 49ers quarterback Colin Kaepernick and the Seahawk's Richard Sherman in their personal element. Commercials show them in their homes, locker rooms and other places most will never get to see them, away from the throngs of fans and the crowds with the simple phrase, "Hear What You Want," spoken like a manifesto. These are the hot new NFL stars that younger fans admire and strive to be one day. They chose athletes that are controversial and viewed by the older generation as rebels or bad boys, but viewed by the younger crowd as cool and fresh. These aren't your dad's headphones, and that's exactly how Beats likes it. Your dad wears Bose, but you love bass so you wear Beats.

Beats isn't the cheapest brand, or the best sounding brand. They are the cool brand. And cool is what teenagers and young people want to be. They want to be fashionable. They want to flaunt. They want to connect with their idols. Beats sells a window into the world of the rich and famous and a chance to connect to music like they do. That's why Beats has the best selling headphones. It's an amazing lifestyle brand.

The Age of the Niche - Go Small Or Go Home

We live in the age of the niche and micro niche. With more information, there are more and more subsets of people that are discovering their true passion. They are finding out what really makes themselves tick and the possibilities are nearly endless. At the same time, the world's population is yearning for brands and products to identify with. They want products that are tailored or made just for them (or at least they seem that way). How many times have you heard some guru's advice start out with, "there are two kinds of people in the world"? They invariably go on to say something really broad and make sweeping generalizations that are just plain wrong. That type of thinking is outdated, and it inevitably degrades a brand because they will soon find out they can't be everything to everyone (and it's no easier to be everything to half the people, either).

The reality is there are millions of types of people out there. There aren't just the jocks and the nerds. There are the jocks who love Crossfit, soccer jocks who follow the Premier League, and the jocks who love one-legged, freshwater-only, nocturnal water skiing. That last one is a stretch, but you get my point. There are tech nerds who are into over-clocking their computers, science nerds who are into advanced super-string theory, comic book nerds that love *Spider-Man*, or environmental nerds who are passionate about turning trash into energy. That last one is true by the way (and very noble in my opinion).

So how can brands capture their niche, and then go beyond their niche and gain mass appeal? I have a theory and it involves what I call the superniche. A superniche is a higher classification that contains all the micro niches. Let's get back to the water sports example.

Imagine I have a great new beverage holder that keeps your drink cool for up to two hours, during even the hottest midsummer days. This groundbreaking invention is targeted to anyone and everyone that wants a cold beverage in the summer months. I decide to take out a full page ad in *USA Today* so my product can get maximum exposure across the widest possible audience. Because my product comes in 5 vibrant colors, I even pay the extra $75,000 to print my ad in color. Great idea, right? I've invested $200,000 in what's sure to be an instant success.

I create an ad I think will appeal to everyone, it has pictures of my product in various settings like pool parties, the beach, the golf course, barbecues and so on. My phone starts ringing the next day, and I'm getting hundreds of hits to my site. The next day I get more calls, but not quite as many as the day before. After a week, the phone has stopped ringing and the sales have petered out. I made $300,000 worth of sales, so decide to run the ad again the next month.

This time, my results weren't so good. The phone rang off and on for a month and my website traffic was down. All told, I only got about a quarter of the response I received the first time. I netted a $125,000 loss.

I'm scratching my head because I'm not sure what went wrong. Maybe I chose the wrong day to run the ad? Maybe there was some bigger news in the paper that captured their attention and they never turned the page? Maybe the ad didn't run in some cities? I call *USA Today* frantic, only for them to tell me that it was just another normal news day, and assurance that the ad had run nationwide.

The next month, I decide to give it one more try. Why not? I'm an optimistic guy. My optimism turns to self pity, when I only get a 10% return on my investment this time. Now I'm furious. I've just lost $180,000 on this ad, in addition to the $25,000 I lost between the first two times I ran it. That's a $215,000 total loss and it had worked so well the first time! How is this possible?

Because my ad was so broadly focused, there is no emotional connection to the readers and no incentive for them to tell their friends. If the product works, that's great. However, only a few of them ever recommend it to their friends because they're not sure if their friends would have any use for it.

It's actually a scenario I see played out all too often. People or companies that have a great product or service try to jump right into the ocean without first testing out the waters of all the little pools in their neighborhood. Like an overnight pop star with a catchy hit single, they get massive success that quickly dwindles and is not sustainable.

Great brands are shifting their focus. They are capturing smaller audiences that will lead to the more mainstream superniche. Then and only then, they begin to attack the wider marketplace in hopes of striking broader fame and mass appeal. It happens all the time on YouTube, and innovative brands are starting to take notice. Just think of all those YouTube stars who now have their own talk shows, reality shows and albums.

Here's how I could have marketed my product and ultimately my brand to capitalize on our current world of the niche:

I know my beverage holder is great for everyone but I first decide to go after the water sports enthusiasts. I send a few of my reps to the national championships and set up a booth. I bring only one color of my beverage holder, blue, because I know that blue is the color that they most connect with. I get a few of the pro water skiers to wear my logo on their uniform in exchange for $500 dollars. The booth costs only another $500, because it's a relatively small affair but about 2,000 people show up in the stands. I have a few of my staff dress up in water skiing suits and pass out 2,000 of my beverage holders to the crowd, telling them this is THE beverage holder dedicated to water skiers. It was manufactured with the water sports enthusiasts in mind.

While they retail for $9.99, it really only costs me $2.00 to produce, so my total product cost is $4,000. All told, with expenses getting to and from the event and paying my staff to be there, I'm out about $10,000.

An amazing thing happens though. The event-goers really like my product. They connect with my product on a more personal and emotional level because this product was made for them and my staff dresses like they do. About 5% of the people snap a picture and upload it to their social media profile. That's 100 people repping my product. Each of them has 300 friends and followers on average, so my product reaches a minimum of

30,000 people who are passionate and interested about what their friends are into. Of those 30,000, 7% of the people decide to buy my product, because they are also into water sports. At our $9.99 price point, we've now taken in $21,000—or a $11,000 profit.

I do the same thing at a fishing tournament with my green colored beverage holder. I tell the fisherman and fans in attendance that my beverage holder was intended for all water sports and this green one in particular was made for the fisherman community. My staff wears fisherman vests and hats. The same thing happens over and over again as I approach the yachting community, the surfing crowd and so on. After about a year sales are pouring in from every sub niche of my superniche, the water sports community. That, in essence is how you reach a superniche and more mass appeal by starting with a micro niche. Sometimes brands get really lucky and those niches blow up.

Tweet the Deets:
Sustainable success in today's economy comes from capturing the micro niche. #MovingTargets

Interview with Joey Redner, Founder of Cigar City Brewery

Cigar City Brewery burst onto the budding craft beer scene in 2009. Its founder, Joey Redner has a passion for brewing the highest quality beers, and the world's critics agree. Cigar City won Gold at the National Beer Championships and The Great American Beer Festival, and the beer connoisseur website RateBeer.com rated Cigar City the 4th best brewery in the world in 2013. Yes, that's right, the world. They had the good fortune of being at the right place at the right time when the craft beer industry exploded, and have built a multimillion dollar brand. I had the wonderful opportunity to pick Joey's brain on brand strategy.

Gabe: CCB is known for throwing events where you introduce beers and interact with your customers and fans. What emphasis do you place on connecting with brand enthusiasts and why is it so important to you?

Joey: We put a lot of focus on the hardcore beer geek. Mostly because I consider myself a beer geek and I opened CCB with that mindset. And we have a lot of beer geeks working here. As we have grown our business model has begun to look very different than when we opened, but I am still a beer geek at heart. I still get geeked out about the kinds of beers most beer drinkers seldom buy. 90% of the beer we make falls into the core/seasonal category, but as a company we still get very excited about the more esoteric stuff.

Gabe: Good brands do things differently from the norm. Your beer comes in cans rather than bottles. Can you tell me the thinking behind that decision?

Joey: We started out exclusively in bottles, but that was really a financial decision. I couldn't afford to can. The barrier to entry for cans used to be very high. Cans, to me, are more practical and they take light completely out of the equation so once we could afford to can our beers we dived head first into it.

Gabe: Admittedly craft beer has become a hot trend in the U.S. In your opinion, how can brands capitalize on trends without losing their soul?

Joey: Keep it real. Remember the why. I started CCB to make beer I wanted to drink. If you stay true to the why and do the work, most of the time, good things happen as a result. We have a Director of Keeping It Real, Chris Lovett and one of his jobs is to make sure our walk matches our talk in everything we do. It is his job to pipe up, lovingly, and call us on it if we are doing shit we shouldn't be doing.

Gabe: Stories connect consumers to brands. CCB crafts not only great beer, but compelling stories that go along with them. What makes a great story and why do you think it works?

Joey: A great story to me sheds a little more light on a time or place. It adds the "why" to the "what." Tampa has a unique history. It really mirrors the American melting pot story with immigrants from very diverse cultures bringing their shared experiences and creating something new in a new place. Having that in your backyard and knowing the story hasn't been told to a wider audience is an opportunity. I think most people like having a deeper understanding of the history behind a place. Certainly most craft beer drinkers I have met do. Some cities do it better than others, New Orleans, New York, San Francisco, etc. But, there are compelling stories all over the world that can add to the appreciation of a place.

Gabe: You have a number of beers that you keep small, they are special releases that never reach large distribution. They are reserved for your truly passionate fans and those that visit the brewery. How can creating a limited edition product for a subset of your consumer actually build esteem and more buzz for a brand than saturating the market?

Joey: Most beer geeks are promiscuous by nature. They want to try something new rather than drink their 5th of the same beer in a row. I am very much that way; I hop all over the place when I am drinking beer. But, the beer geek population is small in the grand scheme of things. Small, but influential. They tend to be major influencers in their circle of friends and family. If they see a brewery truly does have passion they will carry the torch for them, even if they are only occasional purchasers of their product. As a brewery if you get geeked out about creating new things rather than just making the same core beers over and over that aligns very nicely with the drinking habits of that small, but influential, segment of craft beer drinkers who want to explore new ground with you.

Since the market for most beer styles—especially higher alcohol, sour or more experimental types—is relatively small, the limited release model works nicely. That said, as consumer taste changes I expect that some styles that have typically been smaller batch will grow in volume. I think lower-alcohol sours have that potential.

Gabe: In your opinion, what is the best way to seek out and then capitalize on a niche market?

Joey: The best way is to really understand it. To have a real passion, real love for it. You can't fake it. You have to really be a fan yourself.

Gabe: Winning awards really sky-rocketed your brand and put it on the map in a short amount of time. What lessons would you give to brands to manage massive success that comes quickly?

Joey: The most important thing is to stay true to the goal. We didn't always put our best face forward when we were growing and it took a concerted effort to slow down and remember the quality matters more than the quantity. There are important lessons that need to be learned during the process of growth and if you skip those lessons you are bound to regret it.

Gabe: What are some of the challenges a brand like yours faces when they want to break out onto the national scene?

Joey: The further you get from home the less you resonate. That is why story is so important. You have to introduce yourself in a new market. You have to go back to startup mode and tell your story over and over, and the further away you get from your backyard the harder that is to do. If you make a good product it is easier, but good alone isn't enough. You have to make a connection.

CHAPTER 13

LET'S PLAY A GAME

Gamification is the newest buzzword in the marketing and branding world right now. In truth, it's a concept that has been around since the beginning of commerce. When you were a kid did you ever get that Baskin Robbins punch card where you buy 9 ice creams and get the 10th one free? If you answered yes, then you've been gamified! If you have ever participated in a frequent flyer program in hopes of getting a free ticket you've played the ultimate version of gamification. In fact, when you play the airlines' game for long enough, it's not even about the free ticket anymore, it's about the status and being able to say you are Platinum Elite Club Super Member of the Millennium, or whatever they're calling it now.

Everyone loves a good game, and that's why it can be such a powerful branding tool. The great thing about games is that the incentive doesn't have to break the bank. It's the joy of the game itself that captures people's attention. It's a way to break the monotony of their day. It plays on the primal instinct to win.

In today's world, gamification has gone to a new level truth be told. There is even a social network, Foursquare, dedicated to the concept where you can "check in" and ultimately become "mayor" of your favorite bar, attraction or business. Various achievements and "badges" can be unlocked. For instance, ten check-ins will earn a user the "Greasy Spoon" badge. Some restaurants or bars will even offer a free drink or appetizer with the first Foursquare check-in. This way—for the price of a bottle of IPA or a bowl of edamame—all of that customers' Foursquare friends will see where they are eating or drinking, and likely read a favorable comment about the restaurant's free booze, too. With smartphones now in everyone's pocket, gamification can be taken to new heights and played around the clock.

Gamification is a way brands can interact with their own employees and customers in a fun way in order to build loyalty. Companies use gamification to boost productivity by offering incentives, badges and other awards to employees who complete certain tasks within the workplace. Brands use it to get customers more actively involved and to share a brand message to their friends via social media.

You only need to look at the explosion of the video game market to know why gamification has become a big trend. Video games are no longer the sole domain of the youth. According to Entertainment Software Association's 2013 study, the average age of a gamer is 31 years old. More interesting still, the average age of the most frequent game purchaser is 35 and the average gamer has been playing for 14 years or more. You might be also shocked to find out that gaming is not just a male pastime. Believe it or not, 48% of all gamers are women. All told the video gaming industry is a $21.5 billion behemoth surpassing movie box office revenue numbers by 100%.

If you want to get really meta, Microsoft's Xbox Live gaming network has incorporated gamification into the video games themselves—players complete tasks to unlock various achievements in a video game, thereby increasing a kind of overall "Gamer Score." What do these gamer points do? Absolutely nothing! But people will play a game for hours just to unlock a unique achievement badge, and my friends and I scoff at "noob" online gamers with Gamer Scores that are in the cellar. It's a game within a game, and it makes the head spin to think about it.

Grow Financial is a bank that knows branding, and knows the value of gamification as well. Their ads take an everyman approach, using quirky-voiced narrators instead of the booming announcer voice, and they have mastered the art of human connection. They use gamification with savings accounts for children, which they call the "Bugg Club". Every time a child makes a deposit of $10 or more, they earn a stamp. If the child makes five deposits his five stamps earn him a gift from the treasure box in the bank. This very simple game helps kids learn the valuable fiscal lessons of saving, endears parents to the brand and creates bank customers for life.

Games play to our most base desires as humans and that's why they work. The natural desire for praise and accolades from peers can be served by earning badges and gold stars that can be put on display. The innate need for exploration can be accomplished by things like scavenger hunts. The inborn thirst to win is quenched by point systems and a leaderboard. The inclination to stretch beyond ourselves is reached by completing challenges and attaining new levels. All this and more is achieved with gamification.

Interview with Benjamin Kosinski, Founder of Sumpto

I had the pleasure of speaking with Benjamin Kosinski, founder of Sumpto. com, a brand that exemplifies the gamified experience. Sumpto leverages the power of social media by rewarding college students with merchandise and other swag from top brands in exchange for them posting sponsored content and photos on their Facebook and Twitter accounts. For each message they post, the student earns points toward a reward which is tracked within the website. It's a win-win for the students who get free goodies and the advertisers who have powerful influencers promoting their brand message.

Gabe: Tell me a little history on Sumpto and how you came up with the concept.

Benjamin: I had a really unique college experience, playing two years of college basketball at a very small school in Massachusetts called Clark University. I was unemployed in my sophomore year, so I decided to transfer to a University in Miami where I joined a fraternity. It was a completely different school, with completely different types of students. The one thing I noticed that was synonymous between the two was how connected to each other college students were online, and essentially how much untapped peer-to-peer influence existed within our online conversations. When I graduated a couple years ago, I saw the difficulties brands had in reaching the college demographic. So then I asked "what if we could identify these trend setters on campus and let them organically do the talking for the brands on line?"

Gabe: Gamification is the buzz word right now, so tell me: why do you think games are so captivating and why are they getting so much attention?

Benjamin: I think that it goes back to the psychology of humans. We constantly want to complete things and we want to be rewarded for our actions. So if a website or a service can really find that trigger, or can find some way to get a user to perform a certain task on their website by rewarding them—through games, or incentives, or simply the gamification aspect— then there's a lot of benefit for that website and anyone else who is involved with that platform.

Gabe: So what are some of the characteristics or concepts that actually make for a good game?

Benjamin: I think there always has to be a trigger... there has to be an incentive and there has to be a clear line of how people would get from that trigger and be rewarded with that incentive. So you have to show the user what they can win, or what they can achieve, or what can happen if they complete that task. And try to make it as seamless and as easy as possible.

If you are able to combine that with a community feel, or able to make it seem to the user that, "hey, if you don't do this task, there are a thousand other people who will"…and then also if you do this task, you are gaining experience…I think that's a very good way to go about it. So, it's really about combining the group mentality that humans have inherently with an incentive.

Gabe: What ways do you think brands can capitalize on gamification—taking those concepts with the triggers that you mentioned, and actually developing fans and ultimately customers for their brand?

Benjamin: I think a lot of them are trying to become content creators. So they are trying to have users create all this User Generated Content on behalf of the brand, and they can push it off to their own channels. Having these incredible word-of-mouth recommendations from these brand advocates is a lot more effective, and a lot more meaningful than just the brands giving out these traditional ads. Some things that brands can do is offer an incentive, but at the same time have these users complete a series of tasks to get that incentive, and really try to make it into either a gamified process or competitive process. While doing that, it kind of naturally filters out the people who really want that product and want to be connected with that brand, and the people who are also just kind of shrugging it off; so that natural filter allows brands to easily identify these potential brand advocates and loyalists.

Gabe: When you're developing a game that will capture people's attention for the brand, what advice would you give to brands starting out that want to start creating their own games?

Benjamin: I think you need to understand the actual over-arching goal of the program. You need to know who you want to connect with. Just putting it out there in general, I don't think that is the best approach. I really think exclusivity, or something unique and that a lot of people are attracted to is key. So for Sumpto, it's all about college— that kind of exclusivity, that community feel is built into our platform. I really think that people respond inherently well to communities and exclusivity. I also think that there needs to be a relationship between these brands and their potential consumers, or users, whatever it may be. It's a lot more valuable to create a meaningful relationship on a one-to-one basis rather than just trying to scale an approach to any and everyone. So almost a hand-holding approach for brands with their potential users is a good way to start off, and then you can easily find the champions, the advocates, the loyalists for your brand by including gamification, and inserting these competitive nature-based contests into the potential programs.

Gabe: Gamification is all about increasing engagement. What ways have you seen games take brands to a new level in engaging their target audiences?

Benjamin: The first thing that comes to mind, and maybe one of the first sites that did it really well was LinkedIn. When LinkedIn started a couple of years ago, they were one of the first ones to really emphasize the percentage of the profile you completed. When you saw that your LinkedIn profile was only about 30% complete, you didn't want to see that line *only* filled about 30% of the total it could possibly be. You wanted to complete your tasks because you knew the reward if you complete your profile by 10 *more* percent was that your profile could get seen by hundreds of thousands of more people. This was all achieved by simply putting in your hometown or putting in your major in college, and that was a really unique way for LinkedIn to do several things: create more engagement among the users, understand more about those users and have them complete their information. This inherently increases everyone's user experience, as well.

So we use that on some Sumpto for users own profiles and it's kind of inherent nature; they really just want to complete those tasks so they can see that 100% completion level on that profile.

Gabe: Yes, there's something to be said for a reward system as well, I'm sure. At what point does a game really cross over from being something fun or whimsical to actually making an impact? Where is that line and how do brands get there?

Benjamin: You know, I don't know if you really even want to find the line. I think it's supposed to be fun and whimsical, and if it's too serious, if it's too forced then people aren't going to respond well to it. They should feel they are almost not playing a game. If you're able to create a real gamified experience, or a really cool competitive nature online through our co-program, then all the other benefits will just accrue naturally. I think the end goal should be just to create the user's experience or generate a better user experience for those people on the website. While doing so, you'll get all the benefits that come along with that.

Gabe: That makes total sense. How have you transformed the users into players? So what channels do you use to get people playing, and what avenues would you recommend brands explore if they are trying to get started with gamification?

Benjamin: Well, there are basic social groupings in college. So college is inherently social, and by that I mean that there are so many groups on campus and there are so many different ways for people to be a part of groups. You know them by colleges, by fraternities and sororities, which house you live in, which dorm you live in, your classes; everything is grouped into these little sub-communities. So we're able to play off those existing components and apply it to our websites in a very natural and seamless way. As we try to minimize the friction points along that, that just enhances the user experience.

For brands and for other people trying to really implement gamification, I think it's an understanding you use the basics ... understanding what is a natural trigger. So for college students, people love bragging about their school. My school is better than your school, your school's football team is not as good as mine. Whatever, awesome, great! Fraternities and sororities, different groups and organizations, those are natural triggers within the college demographic that they were able to apply. But for every user base, there's always those existing groups and our existing connections. And if you're able to leverage those existing connections on your platform, then that will create some really cool competitive engagement.

Gabe: How do you keep a game from becoming stale? In what ways do you change the game to keep it interesting once you see the engagements declining?

Benjamin: I think you need to constantly change it up...but you don't want to change it up too much that people are like, "wow I'm never gonna be able to win." You don't want to dangle it in front of their face forever and have them never be able to touch it. You want them to be able to get from point A to point B, and then when they get to point B, then they are saying "wait, there's also point C." Once they get to C they're saying "oh wait I can also get to point D." But I think if you kind of push it and say "hey, look you can get from point A to point Z" people will say "that's such a huge task I don't want to do all that, it's gonna take me so long."

By minimizing the time frame and giving them incentives that they can easily and quickly achieve, that is the best way to do it. And then once they achieve, you tell them "hey you can also win this," or "you can also perform these tasks" and that will really keep the engagement going on a prolonged time period. But I think staging is very critical for a user in understanding that they can actually achieve that goal in a certain time period—and then once they achieve it there is more that they can actually get.

CHAPTER 14

STORIES CONNECT PEOPLE

"No, no! The adventures first, explanations take such a dreadful time."
-Lewis Carroll

Storytelling is the universal pastime that connects all societies. People love a great story no matter their culture, creed or income bracket. Ever since the first Grandpa Caveman began spinning a tall tale by the campfire, people have been innately drawn to the narrative process. Today's best brands don't just tell us who they are and what they do, they manage to craft a gripping story that captures your full attention. The best stories do all the selling for the brand because they put potential customers into an emotional state of mind. It's in the emotional state that purchases happen.

Here's a great quote from Peter Guber, chairman and CEO of Mandalay Entertainment that I think translates really well to the subject of modern branding:

"Today everyone, whether they know it or not, is in the emotional transportation business. More and more, success is won by creating compelling stories that have the power to move people to action. Simply put, if you can't tell it, you can't sell it."

I encourage you to tell the story of your brand in a way that will resonate with your avatar or niche. The story should be in your brochures and collateral, on your website and throughout your print and multimedia ads. Today's consumer thinks what you do is boring. They can find what you sell somewhere else. So give them what they can't find down the road or on another site: a compelling narrative filled with passion and humanity.

If you don't have a story to tell, don't be afraid to make one up. One of the best brand campaigns I've seen in recent years was completely fabricated. Dos Equis' "The Most Interesting Man in the World" is a jewel of storytelling wrapped into easily digestible 30 second bites. The Most Interesting Man, who remains anonymous, is seen living a passionate life of adventure and decadence throughout the ads. Some of my favorite one-liners from the campaign include: "When he drives a new car off the lot, it increases in value." "Cuba imports cigars from him." "He lives vicariously through himself."

At the end of each ad, the Most Interesting Man makes the poignant statement, "I don't always drink beer, but when I do, I prefer Dos Equis." It's a tongue-in-cheek stab at themselves which is brilliant. They leave the selling up to the story.

In an interview with Fast Company, Jonathan Goldsmith, the actor that portrays the Most Interesting Man stated, "I think the campaign is so successful, because every man, including me, would like to be like him."

It wasn't just men who liked the campaign though. The videos went viral. Sales of the beverage skyrocketed, and Dos Equis became the fastest growing beer import into the U.S. That's the power of a great story.

Here are some tips to keep in mind when crafting a great brand story:

- Make sure your story is relevant to your target audience. It can be about you, but in the end it needs to be about them.

- Be mindful of your tone. Amusing is great if you want your brand to be lighthearted (think MailChimp), but just make sure it aligns with your industry. Lawyers, accountants, and the like wouldn't get the same response from humor as a tech company. They would be better served with a more dramatic or historical approach in most cases.

- Don't be afraid to get personal. People will connect with you more closely if you do. Just don't be too self righteous or self glorifying.

- Everyone loves a struggle. If your brand has had obstacles or challenges to overcome, don't be afraid to tell that story. All of the greatest stories must have an element of conflict.

- If you don't have a compelling story to tell, gather testimonials from your customers or clients. Tell the story from their perspective on how your product or service has changed their life.

CHAPTER 15

BUILDING ON A STRONG FOUNDATION

In the world of branding there are four characteristics your brand must have. Each of these qualities may be weighted differently, but missing one or more of these four traits will limit your success. I like to call these qualities the four pillars of branding. These pillars are differentiation, relevance, esteem, and knowledge.

Differentiation

Differentiation, simply put, is what sets you apart. Are you sleeker, faster, sexier, more intuitive? Whatever makes you different from the competition is your brand's first important asset.

Without brand differentiation, the world of business would be a pretty boring place. It would probably look something like Soviet Russia where everyone has a menial task to fill. If you've ever been to a networking meeting or chamber of commerce breakfast and asked someone what they did, only to hear, "I do insurance," you know what I mean. That's usually the time I politely let them know it was a pleasure to meet them and I'm going to get a refill on my coffee.

If the same agent instead announced, "I place busy executives with top tier insurance plans at the lowest premiums in Tampa," they would have a much better shot of getting me interested. Because that's me, I live in Tampa. I'm busy. I want good insurance at the lowest prices. I don't want to search, I want someone else to do the work for me. That's a different pitch than I've ever heard before and I'm intrigued.

There's really no substitute for differentiation. Without it, the rest of the brand pillars just won't bear the weight. Once you have your differentiation, own it—and milk it for all it's worth.

My company is the perfect example of a brand that couldn't survive without differentiation. We are a design firm in a sea of tens of thousands of design firms. If I were to approach prospects and tell them we can design it better or for less money, it wouldn't hold any credence. Big deal. There are probably more talented designers and cheaper design firms out there.

What makes us special is that we are *the* design firm for golf clubs and country clubs. We know the industry inside and out. We have a track record of success and countless testimonials from our clients who are golf and country clubs. Our portfolio is filled with great graphic design that features the clubs we represent.

Relevance

It's great to be different, but if you're not different in a relevant way it doesn't mean a heck of a lot. Relevance is what *matters* to the consumer of your brand. There a tons of products on store shelves that are different, but if they're not different in a relevant way, they are left to compete on price or placement.

If you needed to mail a package and walked into your local post office to see a brown box for $2.99 and a white box with the same dimensions and build quality for $3.29 you would inevitably choose the brown one right? There's no relevant difference to most people. The box is a means to an end quite literally.

Now what if you had something fragile and valuable to mail like a watch? If there was a plain brown envelope for $1.99 but next to it sat a padded white envelope, that difference would be relevant to you.

Esteem and the Red Velvet Rope

Esteem has everything to do with how well regarded you are in the marketplace. Luxury brands like Rolex, Mercedes and Louis Vuitton carry massive esteem. They appeal to a high-end shopper of course, but they appeal to the low-end shopper probably more so. That's because esteem and ambition go hand in hand.

However, esteem isn't just limited to the luxury space. Brands can be esteemed for their charitable giving, as well. Take the shoe brand Tom's, which donates a pair of their shoes to the less fortunate for each pair purchased by consumers. A brand can also be esteemed for creating unique and alternative work environments where employees thrive, like Google. Celebrity endorsement is a fast track to esteem, but the hardest and costliest to achieve in most cases.

Limiting accessibility is a strong way brands can generate esteem. When Google's email platform, Gmail, was launched, access was only granted to a few influencers. They were then allowed to send up to 10 invites. Gmail had so much esteem that people were selling them on Ebay, and trading them on Craigslist. Nightclubs in every major city do the same thing. The red velvet rope is the penultimate symbol of esteem. Those on the inside have what it takes and the others are left on the other side (or so they'd have you think, anyway).

On a similar note, limiting production or creating limited editions is a fast track to esteem. Nike does it with sneakers, Chanel does it with perfume, Rolex does it with watches—even magazines sell more issues by printing multiple limited editions with a different (and often regionally-targeted) athlete/celebrity on each cover. By reducing production, brands like these create insatiable desire.

Knowledge

Our last pillar of branding is knowledge. Having exceptional differentiation, relevance and esteem for your brand is wasted without it. If nobody knows who you are it won't matter how much of the other brand attributes you have.

Knowledge is the place where branding collides with good PR and marketing. The best of which is word of mouth. Malcolm Gladwell, in his book *The Tipping Point,* showed that finding influencers is the shortcut to word of mouth success that leads to epidemics of all kinds, including buzz. If you can get your brand in front of these people, the word can spread like wildfire.

One of the most notorious examples of this is when rapper Snoop Dogg wore a Tommy Hilfiger shirt during a musical performance on *Saturday Night Live* in the mid-90s. The next Monday, teens and young adults from every corner of the United States were rocking Tommy Hilfiger polos, and the brand went on to become one of the biggest must-have wardrobe essentials in hip hop.

The Influencers

The Tipping Point shows how brands don't need to reach the masses individually. By finding a few influential people who can generate buzz, your brand can go from unknown to warp speed. Gladwell's influencers include:

"The Connector" - These are the people that know *everyone*. They are masters at putting people from all walks of life and industry together. They cross-pollinate from every corner of the country or planet, forging relationships and partnerships of all kinds.

"The Maven" - These are the people that have a passion for sharing their knowledge and experience with others. Most often, they do it for unselfish reasons. They want to spread the word and help others make better decisions. They love to be cutting and even bleeding edge, and are often early adopters. They get their kicks by spreading the gospel of your brand.

"The Salesman" - These are the people with magnetic personalities. When they talk, people listen and they might not even know why. They have the "it" factor. Salesman can persuade their friends and anyone else they come into contact with in a short amount of time.

The Power of the Champion

I would like to add my own influencer to this list: the champion. The champion is someone your brand has touched in a deep and meaningful way. Brand champions can come from within or from the outside and they are someone you help to create, they just might need a little push. Champions will spread your message and connect you to everyone they know because of the impact you made on them. I would argue that they offer the most palpable form of brand buzz.

One way to create a brand champion is by paying it forward. It is truly the law of reciprocity in action. Doing something meaningful for someone else elicits a desire to return the favor. Oftentimes, that person will pay it back in multiples. It's important to remember that champions are created through actions with genuine motivations. People will see through it if you do it to for selfish reasons, expecting a return. Do good for others, and good will come.

Another way to create brand champions is to show them what's in it for them. I've built brand champions who pushed my products and services up the ranks in their organization for me because they wanted to be the hero for their company and wanted to be in the spotlight. It's a natural human desire to be recognized and rewarded. Show people why your product or service will do that for them and give them the exclusive.

Case Study in Brand Personality - Courtyard by Marriott

On a recent trip to Wilmington, North Carolina for a wedding I had the pleasure of staying at the brand new Courtyard by Marriott Downtown Historic District. I hadn't stayed at a Courtyard property in many years, so I approached my stay from a fresh perspective of their brand.

From the minute I drove up, I was greeted by helpful and friendly staff that addressed me and my family like we were the most important guests they had ever had stay there. The first thing that struck me as different was that when I handed my keys to the valet attendant, he told me the first names of the two staff members at the front desk and how they would take great care of me. By mentioning their first names, I felt like this was a cohesive team that enjoyed working with one another and, in turn, would give me personal attention.

That feeling of cohesion was heightened when the front desk staff delivered on that promise. They asked me questions about my trip, explained my options for exploring the hotel and the city and asked me what needs I had.

The hotel was only two months old when I arrived. The lobby and rooms sported a modern decor filled with vibrant colors and interesting patterns on the walls, bed coverings and furniture. You could tell that whomever designed the place really put care and thought into every detail. On a purely aesthetic level it was a solid 9 out of 10 for me. The extra care they put into the decor showed me that my visual experience was important for them.

Beyond the aesthetics, the friendly personality of their brand was evident throughout, right down to the signage of the hotel. The classic "Do Not Disturb" door hanger was replaced by one that read, "I need some me time." Written below it in a smaller typeface was, "Please do not disturb." I noted how they put the customer first, and did so in a personal way, by describing it the way they did. "Me time," I thought to myself, how relaxing.

When I called to the front desk requesting a crib for my infant son, they weren't sure they had one, but told me they would search for one and let me know. A few minutes later, a courteous young lady told me they had found one and told me the name of a gentleman who would be right up to deliver it. I was surprised to find it was not maintenance personnel or a bellhop, but the front desk manager himself who delivered it to me. That showed me that no one there was above doing menial jobs if it meant exceptional customer experience. He then handed me a bag filled with little bath toys, treats and soaps for the baby which was totally above and beyond and showed me profits weren't their only motivation.

Throughout our few days there the ladies at the front desk would rush over when we got off the elevator to stalk and play with my son in his carriage. They even gave him little treats for the trip home on our last day there.

If I ever visit Wilmington again I will stay at that hotel. If I ever hear of someone traveling there, I will tell them to stay at the Courtyard Downtown. The day I got back home I went to TripAdvisor and wrote them a fantastic review. They built a loyal brand champion that day, and they did it the right way. They were personal, tasteful, a team, caring, selfless and gave me something for nothing.

How to Get a Reaction

So you've just created the world's best product or service. Now what? What makes a brand a brand is what comes next.

Keep It Clear

Today's savvy consumer doesn't play games. They can cut through the B.S. and gimmicks. They reward honesty and are quick to judge companies with shady practices, and they'll be sure to let the world know about it at the same time.

Today's consumer wants consistent and clearly marked pricing from your brand. You would think by now, in the developed world, that is obvious and not even worth mentioning. Well, it's not and it is. There are still snake oil salesman, bait and switch gimmicks and all manner of underhanded practices.

There's a rose vendor that sets up on weekends near my home. Every weekend they put out their crudely drawn sign to proclaim "Roses, $8 / doz." On Mother's Day and other "flower" holidays it goes up to $15. It's a clear attempt to bilk money out of the consumer because they can. They don't even try to hide it. They just post a piece of cardboard slapped over the regular price. Some might remark that they have a keen sense of capitalism. I call it price gouging. It's a leftover third-world practice that doesn't belong in today's world and is seen for what it is, misguided opportunism. I boycott the place, and I'm not alone.

Could you imagine walking into a McDonalds on Labor Day to find all the burgers were double the price? It doesn't fly. In fact, there would probably be a riot.

Gas stations have been pulling the 9/10ths scam for a while, but now they've taken it a step further. Many service stations advertise a gasoline price on their display board, but if you look closely there is "Cash Only" written in the fine print. Guess what, I don't go to those stations anymore. I'm not alone.

I've noticed convenience stores pulling a similar tactic. On a recent trip to Boca Raton I stopped in a mini mart for a bottle of water and a snack. The clerk rang me up and told me the price was "$4.75. I reached in my pocket and when I produced cash, he told me "Ah, wait a moment, that's $3.92." He probably thought I would be happy, but it actually pissed me off. I'll never stop there again.

Those tactics only erode your perceived value and consumer confidence and are detrimental to your brand. Good brands keep their pricing clearly marked in store and on their site. Good brands are open and up front. That instills trust and is a much stronger long-term strategy. Quick gains are rarely worth it in the long run, and never worth it in the world of brand building.

Humor

Humor can be an impactful way for a brand to expand their message. It's not a good fit for every brand, but for those who get it right, the results can be astonishing. The reason it works well for some brands is because it gives life to otherwise boring subject matter.

The Dollar Shave Club is a prime example. Who gets excited about buying razors? Their viral video (which currently has 15 million views as of this book) sure got people's attention with its quick witted one liners that told a compelling story of how the owner and his immigrant assistant would ship great razors to your door for a dollar a month. You don't need fancy shave tech, just simple affordable quality. A costumed bear even shows up in the commercial. It's comedy genius, and the country ate it up. Great humor gave their brand life.

Consistency

Consistency is the key that unlocks trust in the consumer. Good brands keep everything from their colors to the smell of their storefront homogenous, because they know that consistency will lead to an expectation. That expectation, in turn, leads to trust and eventually to sales.

Consistency > Expectation > Trust > Sales > Repeat Business
& Word of Mouth

If we look at the converse, we see the same principles hold true but the result is far different. Brands that don't provide a consistent look and customer experience create no expectation. When there is no expectation there is mistrust and declining sales follow because there is no repeat business. There is, however, word of mouth, but not the kind brands are looking for.

The worst thing you can be to your customer is "hit or miss." People are always quicker to criticize than give praise, so you can expect to get exponentially worse buzz for all the times you miss.

Inconsistency > Lack of Expectation > Lack of Trust > Declining Sales > No Repeat Business & Unwanted Word of Mouth

There was a time in my life that I was stranded on a desert island. Well, sort of. The reality is that it was an island of my choosing, and pretty lush and scenic. I lived on a small island called Siquijor (pronounced see-key-hor) in the Philippines that is a dot on a map, if it's even on the map at all. It is the most remote place I have ever been by a long run (and believe me, I have found myself in some strange places).

The island is 63 miles in circumference and comprised of 80,000 residents or so. On the side of the road they sold what I liked to call green Coke. You wouldn't want to drink it though, because it's not Coke at all— it's actually gasoline stored in 1 liter Coca-Cola bottles. In fact, there were only a couple of proper gas stations on the island. It was for exactly that type of reason that I lived there though. Siquijor had no malls, no heavy traffic and certainly no fast food joints.

The closest island I would consider "civilization" was an hour and half boat ride away. It was a small city called Dumaguete on an island called Negros. Dumaguete sported a lot more congestion, a tiny mall that was actually just one big department store, and the holy grail of American fast food: a McDonalds restaurant.

My days in Siquijor were filled with rice for breakfast, rice for lunch and rice for dinner. The topping might have changed, but the presentation was the same. After a few months, my heart would yearn and my stomach would beg for a double cheeseburger and fries. Maybe a chicken nugget or two. Definitely for some non banana-based ketchup. I would make the trek across the choppy waters of the archipelago for some excuse or another that was hiding the fact I craved something, anything American.

And guess what? McDonalds came through, and met my expectation, each and every time. I would argue it tasted even better than it does in the States, but I'll chalk that up to fiendish desire. The fact is, it tasted the same. Exactly the same. Thousands of miles and decades removed from Ray Kroc's first Des Plaines, Illinois establishment, it tasted, looked, smelled and felt precisely the same. It was comforting to me, so far removed from my home, that I could have the same experience.

That is an extreme example, but it illustrates the power that consistency can have on human emotion.

Some areas your brand should stay consistent:

Visuals
- The size, color and placement of your logo
- Font use and typography
- Ad layouts
- Icons and imagery on social media
- Email signatures of staff
- Business cards and collateral
- Television graphics
- PowerPoint presentation backgrounds and basic layout
- Email blasts / newsletters
- Mobile application icons and graphics

Sound

- Music beds for radio ads, TV ads, video in store / office
- Announcers / Narrator voice type
- Telephone Communications
- The initial greeting
- The persona (cheerful, bright, calm, professional, caring, etc.)
- The sound of voices who answer (man / woman, young / old)

Office / Store

- The decor (retro, modern, distressed, etc.)
- The cleanliness
- The type of music playing
- The smell
- Ambient sounds (the sound of water cascading for instance)

Personnel

- Dress code - Uniformed or not, there shouldn't be t-shirt and jeans mixed with suits and ties.
- Tone of voice taken with customer / client
- Similar personality types (if interacting with customers / clients)

Sales Techniques

If you were reading this book 10 years ago, this chapter would probably end here. I would have told you to keep it consistent, then gave you a pat on your behind and told you to be on your way. But things have changed.

We are in an age of individualism. No one wants a bunch of robots running around. In fact, people want to experience your brand on their terms. They will approach it from different angles and expect to be treated as the individuals they are. People don't like canned responses and auto replies. They don't appreciate formulaic sales funnels.

Consistency in today's world is adaptable. As strange as it sounds, consistency done well makes everyone that interacts with your brand feel special and unique. So how can you go about providing a consistent experience that *seems* different?

Dr. Pepper's ad campaign "I Am", was a genius approach at communicating the message of individualism that could still be serviced by a single product or brand. It featured people from all walks of life and age groups shuffling down the streets, shedding their external garments and adorning shirts that said things like "I'm a dreamer", "I'm a rockstar, "I'm one of a kind" and the like. One man with prosthetic legs runs past wearing an "I'm a fighter" shirt. Another young lady walks past with the only white shirt in a sea of red shirts which proclaims, "I'm a rebel". It ends on a touching note of man handing a woman a Dr. Pepper soda can while she unzips her jacket to reveal the payoff, an "I'm a Pepper" shirt. It was a poignant way to create broad appeal while acknowledging that their customers come in all shapes and sizes.

Some Tips to Stay Consistent to Your Brand Without Being Canned:

In Customer Service: Don't oversimplify your approach. Instead, think big picture and use the core values you have developed to dictate behavior and response. Come up with a set of "if this, then that" scenarios and role play them, but don't necessarily write down strict rules of engagement. Train your staff team to learn your system of thinking rather than repetitive rules and answers.

In Sales: It's important to use context. Train yourself and / or your staff to listen to customers and clients with a fresh set of ears. It's easy to "tune out" once you hear a trigger phrase. It's beneficial to have a set of standard objections and corresponding responses, but at the very least try to frame the conversation in the context that makes sense to the client. Try to put your answers in their terminology or jargon. Try to contextualize the story in a practical way they can relate to. This takes practice!

In Print: Know the demographics of the readership of the publication. Craft your ad copy with them in mind. Don't hesitate to adjust your copy for the next one. Be careful to stay true to your brand's voice, though.

On Television: Just as in print, craft the script to cater to the demographics of the channel. Make sure to use the same look and feel and emotion, but you can give it a twist based on who's watching.

In Email Communication / Direct Mail: For one-on-one communication, always address the person by name, even if it takes a few extra seconds to type out.

For mass email blasts or mailings, take the extra step and make sure to auto insert names and relevant information where applicable. Get a good copywriter to make it sound natural. Try to parse through your lists regularly and sub-classify them if possible (and the data is solid).

Also keep in mind that slight modifications to the wording going out to each of your subsets goes a long way to making your brand sound like you're talking to them. For instance, you might take a slightly different approach to men than you would to women. You might speak to older women differently than you would speak to younger women. You say something different to rural women then you would say to metropolitan women, and so on.

In Social Media: Respond directly to people when applicable. Social media is about being social after all. It's not just another platform to speak to the masses. Speaking one-on-one is a powerful way to show you appreciate your customers and prospective customers individually.

CHAPTER 16

ZEROING IN ON YOUR TARGET

What you start out thinking is rarely the conclusion you come to. The same holds true for brand development. Many companies create a product or service with a particular demographic or target audience in mind, only to realize they register with a completely different audience or niche than they expected. Every brand will face this fact to some degree and it's how they handle it that will decide their success or failure. Bad brands get hung up on that sort of thing, while good brands accept it and pivot.

Adaptability is a must for brands in today's world. Take Flickr for instance. Flickr is one of the world's most popular photo sharing platforms. It allows people to upload and share their pictures for the world, but it didn't start out that way exactly.

Flickr's original permutation was an online role playing game where users could buy and sell items and travel along an online map. Photo sharing capabilities were built into the game and it became apparent that it was the most popular feature of the site. Flickr decided to focus on the photo upload and sharing part of their platform, and it took off. They eventually got bought out by Yahoo! for $35 million (which seems small by today's standards but was quite a sum at the time). Brands like Flickr, that are fluid, succeed.

The General Mills brand of cereal, Lucky Charms, made a similar brand pivot. Their research showed that 45% of Lucky Charms eaters were adults, not the children they were exclusively marketing to. Lucky Charms changed their branding and marketing efforts and geared it for their adult buyers in 2012. That year they saw their best sales volume numbers of all time. In hindsight, it makes a lot of sense because kids that loved the cereal eventually grew up, but it was a risky move at the time.

The lesson here is that numbers don't lie. I implore you to take a metric based approach to your brand in the beginning and never stop aggregating data. Accurate data analysis is crucial to building and maintaining your brand, so track *everything*.

Here are some key factors to start tracking:

Who buys from you? - The most obvious thing to start tracking is who is buying, but many brands fail to get specific. The basics include: Are they men or women? What age? What is their average income?

Getting more specific, you might drill down to things like: Do they own their own home? - This might help you determine remarketing campaigns for instance.

Do they share a particular interest? - You might have just found your niche!

What other brands do they buy? - You might realize a secondary product you can offer to fill their needs and wants.

What zip code do they come from? - Helpful for deciding where to place your next billboard or send your direct mail campaign.

Where did they find you? - The obvious use is to help you decide where to direct your marketing dollars. You may find that it's from word of mouth and you should invest more of your time and effort into human assets, or remarketing to past clients or customers.

Don't take responses at face value and make sure to dig for the answer, because the first one you get might not always be accurate. Many an SEO company has taken credit for web traffic that was triggered by another first contact like a billboard or mailing. Plenty of people will tell you they found you from your website, when they first heard about you from someplace else. Social media can also be confused for word of mouth, so make sure to ask in what context their friends told them about you.

What is your rate of repurchase? - Lower numbers could tell you that your customer service is atrocious or there is a broken link in your system. They could also signal that your product was well built and lasts. If your numbers are low investigate more. If it's the latter, combine it with your other data on similar interests and buying habits and consider some products that you can horizontally integrate. If your brand is well regarded, you might be able to capitalize on something new.

Seasonal / Cyclical factors - This is often overlooked by brands that are starting out. Failure to deliver is the one of the worst black eyes that a brand can have. Make sure your product and its distributors are well stocked when the season hits. Conversely, find out when your low periods are and dedicate those times to marketing more aggressively or introducing a complementary product or service that fills the gap during lean times.

CHAPTER 17

HOW TO DEVALUE YOUR BRAND

We've addressed the many things you need to do in today's world to have a successful brand. Now it's time to shift gears and look at things that detract from brand momentum gain. Below are some of the mistakes and some of the poor brand tactics bad companies use, that I recommend you avoid.

Giving Something... With a Catch

I see poorly thought-out marketing campaigns that seem to offer something for free, but turn out to be bait for an info or email grab. My opinion is, if you're going to offer something for free, follow through with it.

This tactic is used all the time with squeeze pages. If you're not familiar with the term, a squeeze page is a website landing page where you offer something of value for prospects like a free ebook, whitepaper or similar and squeeze their email out of them in return, so you can spam them for the rest of time.

The problem with squeeze pages and similar bait and switch tactics are that they leave the prospect with feelings of being used or fooled, and that's the last thing you want to do! The most important moments in the sales process are the first impression and the last impression. If you leave them with a bad taste in their mouth you'll never hear from them again.

Hiding the Goods

Today's world is all about openness and the sharing of ideas. Keeping methods and secrets behind lock and key just doesn't work these days (unless you happen to be Colonel Sanders). People are curious. People want to connect with brands, and they do it by studying the craft.

Take Rolex for instance. They could show the world exactly how each gear moves and each spring reacts, but people will still buy their timepieces. In fact, you can walk down any street in Asia and buy a pretty decent replica that would fool the average person. And yet they still sell watches. That's because they are handmade to exact specifications. They last longer than knockoffs, because they are built with better materials and craftsmanship. All things being equal, their esteem alone would continue to drive sales because there's something in us all that values and appreciates authenticity.

Many brands think that by giving away their special sauce they'll lose their business. In fact, the opposite is true. Give away your knowledge and let people know how you do things, and they will appreciate more deeply the work you put in, and the methods you use—if they're solid. Sure, there are some do-it-yourselfers that will take the knowledge and run with it, but you'll gain many more followers and champions then you'll lose out on.

Remember, we live in an on-demand word where people want service and immediate results. People are more apt to pay for something they know works rather than try to replicate it themselves.

Brands that continue to innovate don't need to worry about copycats anyways, which leads me to my next item.

Resting on Your Laurels

Bad brands are one and done. Good brands continue to add products, invent and push boundaries. Since stagnant brands are quickly forgotten, make sure you dedicate 5 to 10 percent of your energy on exploring new ways to integrate your existing products and services, and development of complementary offerings.

Overcomplicating the Pitch

There's a time and a place for everything. Don't try to stuff it all into your half page ad, 30 second spot or 2 minute presentation.

The initial pitch, whether that's in person, in print or on screen needs to be succinct. Once prospects are intrigued you can begin to peel back the layers and reveal the inner workings. Bad brands, and bad brand designers, don't realize that elegance is born from simplicity. They fill up every inch of the page and packaging with copy and illustration. They muddy up the screen with captions and graphs. They fill sites with images and banners rather than creating an easy to digest story and clear call to action.

Prejudging Prospects

Good brands don't judge. You never know the size of the wallet that is hiding behind those wrinkled and stained trousers, or the pocket book hiding below the frizzy unkempt hair. Preconception is the death of bad brands.

CHAPTER 18

REINVENTION THE RIGHT WAY

Good brands aren't afraid to reinvent themselves. Just ask Pepsi, they've literally gone through four logo changes in the last 20 years, and who knows how many different slogans! Attitudes, desires and tastes change. Brands that stay stagnant quickly lose their moat in today's economy. So how do you make changes for the better without losing who you are? This chapter will help you lay the foundation for systematic sustainable transformation.

People can be very resistant to change, but the good news is that they also tend to adapt quickly. Apple's iOS 7 is a testament to that fact. Apple reinvented their mobile operating system by adopting a flatter design and losing all the texture and gradients from the previous iterations. To be honest, I didn't like the new design, but most did. It became a hot trend in the design world and especially the tech sector. But that's what Apple, a great brand, does.

Your Logo

In general, I would recommend against drastic changes when it comes to your logo. A good designer can make small tweaks like modernizing the typeface or cleaning up the lines and have a huge impact. Your symbol or mark should remain mostly unchanged if you have any brand recognition at all. Curves might need to be adjusted and lines cleaned up, but keep it simple. Colors should remain in the same family, though they can be adjusted to suit modern tastes and palettes.

Your Slogan

Brainstorm words and ideas related to your new brand, its mission, vision, and core values. Three word slogans make the most impact psychologically, but there's no hard and fast rule. I recommend you come up with at least three separate ideas and run them past a focus group of current customers and a sampling of the target markets you will be going after.

Packaging & Collateral

Brand packaging and other collateral materials should be addressed after your logo. Before you get into design elements have a seasoned agency or copywriter re-write the verbiage. The main goals should be external clarity, so approach it from your customer's point of view. Better still, have a focus group test out the new designs and provide feedback.

Website

Again, I would suggest split testing a couple of rough ideas with a focus group. This can be as informal as a few colleagues and friends outside of your company, and as professional as having a firm or consultant arrange an independent analysis. Whichever route you go, make sure the people who are testing fit your target demographic or niche. Very importantly, find people who know your brand and see what their reaction is to the new you.

Web standards and user behavior changes, so make sure you develop the site with current best practices and arrange your navigational elements in a way that is currently accepted. At the time of my writing, that means building your site with mobile responsiveness in mind and eliminating navigation on the left or right side. If you have no idea what I'm referring to, make sure you hire a firm you trust that will help navigate this space for you. Always keep in mind that your new site has a three year life cycle and accept the fact that the web is an ever-changing landscape. Be careful to build your site based on current proven trends, but not on fads.

Your Office or Storefront

A full rebrand involves changing out signage, displays, floor plans and much more. Instead of doing it yourself, I'd suggest getting an interior designer with experience in your industry, who has a keen eye for spotting trends.

Re-train Your Team & Create a Handbook

Create a system of core values if you don't have one, or re-dedicate your brand to them if you do. Getting your team focused on a common goal is a proven way to increase efficiency and output, so make everyone in your company aware of the direction you are heading and why.

It's often useful to provide team members with a handbook that lays out your new philosophy, expectations and goals. Another cool way I've heard some companies approach this is by creating a fun internal video that gets everyone up to speed on the changes.

You may find there are some on your team that are resistant to change. Don't wait to address this or dance around the subject. Let them know you understand that going outside of their comfort zone may be scary, but show them the endgame. If they refuse to change, reclassify their position or get rid of them altogether. You know what they say about rotten apples.

Notify Your Customers

Customers can be very resistant to change and the unknown. Make sure they see it coming, don't just flip the switch on them overnight. Show them where you are going, the reasoning behind your new brand direction and why it's going to be a fun ride. You can do this by a letter, email blast, in-store handout or press release.

Alert the Press

If you've decided to rebrand your business, there's a big reason why. You're either introducing a new product or service, improving on existing ones, you've acquired a new business, you're expanding your market, etc. This is truly newsworthy stuff! At a minimum put out three press releases; one announcing the coming changes, one during the process, and one at completion or grand re-opening.

CHAPTER 19

THE BRAND REPORT CARD

The last thing I would like to convey to you, the entrepreneur, brand manager or marketing executive is this: be authentic. You can take all that other advice and scrap it if you aren't true to yourself first. Brands that stand the test of time have leaders with a clear view of where they are going and why, and who stay true to that focus. They attract the right customers and staff when they can communicate that vision. In this way, branding is a means to an end... but it's a damn fun journey getting there.

I hope you will use this as a guidebook to build the foundation of your brand, but keep in mind that the structure which sits on top will be built with the passion and determination to fulfill your authentic motivation.

It's difficult to step back and evaluate your branding efforts objectively. Branding is ethereal. Sure, sales figures will give you an indication, but they can be influenced by other factors and rarely tell the entire story. With that in mind, this list is my brand report card. You'll know you've done it right when you recognize these characteristics in your brand:

1. You speak your customer's language, and you place yourself on the level of your target audience

2. You provide meaningful interaction, not simply sales pitches

3. You don't oversell, and quite often spend 10% or less of your communication engaging in sales dialogue

4. You don't pretend to be everything to everyone, and you are laser focused in your communication

5. You offer solutions to real problems instead of causing them

6. You are responsive beyond your competition

7. You are quick to correct mistakes, and go above and beyond to make up for failures

8. You have employees that enjoy working for you and you retain your staff longer

9. Your clients and customers are quick to forgive your mistakes

10. You place more value on quality than quantity

I recommend you come back to this list from time to time to check up. Just like an automobile, your brand needs regularly scheduled maintenance. When your brand is firing on all cylinders, you'll not only reach your destination faster—you'll truly enjoy the ride.

ABOUT THE AUTHOR

Gabriel Aluisy is the founder of Shake Creative, a Tampa, Florida based branding and design agency focused on helping country clubs and membership brands build revenue & connect with consumers. He received his bachelor of arts from American University's School of Communication in Washington, DC where he studied Visual Media.

His career began in the film and television industry (most notably working on shows for the Discovery Channel, Spike TV, PBS, and Fox), but soon found his true passion lay in the world of brand development and marketing. After a decade in the industry, he founded Shake Creative with the purpose of combining high end design, affordable pricing and incredible customer service.

He has designed and developed marketing campaigns and brand collateral for over 1,000 companies including national franchises and brands. His work has won awards, but more importantly, has generated millions of dollars of revenue for his clients.

He is passionate about art & design, golf, travel and preserving the world's indigenous cultures & languages. He tweets @GabrielAluisy.

HAVE A BRAND AND WANT TO CONNECT WITH GABRIEL ALUISY AND SHAKE CREATIVE?

SHAKETAMPA.COM

www.ingramcontent.com/pod-product-compliance
Lightning Source LLC
Chambersburg PA
CBHW020837210326
41598CB00019B/1926